GERMAN INVASION PLANS
FOR THE
BRITISH ISLES
1940

GERMAN INVASION PLANS
FOR THE
BRITISH ISLES
1940

Bodleian Library
UNIVERSITY OF OXFORD

This edition reprinted twice in 2007
This edition first published in 2007 by the Bodleian Library
Broad Street Oxford OX1 3BG

www.bodleianbookshop.co.uk

ISBN: 1 85124 356 9
ISBN 13: 978 1 85124 356 3

This edition © Bodleian Library, University of Oxford, 2007
Introduction © Robert Wheeler
Translated from the German by Alastair Matthews

Originally published as *Militärgeographische Angaben über England, 1940.*

Designed by Dot Little

Printed and bound by The University Press, Cambridge

British Library Cataloguing in Publication Data
A CIP record of this publication is available from the British Library

CONTENTS

Introduction

As England, in spite of her hopeless military situation, still shows no willingness to come to terms, I have decided to prepare, and if necessary to carry out, a landing operation against her. The aim of this operation is to eliminate the English mother country as a base from which the war against Germany can be continued and, if it should be necessary, to occupy it completely. – Adolf Hitler[1]

On 21 June 1940, the French government under Marshal Pétain signed an armistice with Germany. Britain stood alone. The greater part of the British Expeditionary Force had been evacuated from Dunkirk but was exhausted and had left behind its equipment. Churchill had declared that Britain would never surrender, but many observers thought that some form of accommodation with Germany was inevitable.

At the end of June, the German military started to prepare plans for an invasion. German army doctrine decreed that the first stage in the production of such plans should be a military-geographical assessment. This was issued on 15 August, though its findings will have been available earlier. It was one of the bulkiest of such studies by the Army General staff, running to three portfolios. Portfolio A comprised a description of the country as a whole, accompanied by a booklet of photographs and a sheaf of maps; Portfolio B focused on London; Portfolio C provided views of the coast to facilitate the selection of invasion beaches. Subsequently a compilation of 'military objects' was added. These were facilities of military importance, which might be regarded as targets if held by opposing forces or as key points if held by own forces. This edition provides a translation of much of the text from Portfolio A, illustrated by photographs and map extracts taken from the whole of the study.

The study followed a standard pattern. An initial description of the country is followed by a short account of its political organisation. An account of its physical geography, climate, rivers and settlement patterns follows – this is omitted here as being not significantly different from numerous other such accounts. A description of its economy is more revealing as an indication of what the Germans were interested in. There follows a description of the transport system: the state of the road network was an important factor in the selection of invasion routes. A description of communications networks – radio, telephone and telegraph – has been omitted as being of specialist interest and not influencing the military conclusions. Then comes an account of social conditions, as the authors perceived them. Finally, the whole is evaluated from a military perspective.

This is followed by short accounts of each region. These have been compressed here but the military evaluation of each is retained in full. Last, a collection of useful phrases is given, with notes on English weights and measures – a topic which seems to have confused even the compilers.

The conclusions of the study point to the relative unsuitability of Kent for a landing – the Medway provided a natural barrier which the defenders could exploit – and favoured the central south coast. This appears to have been taken into account in the earliest plans for *Operation Sea Lion*, as the invasion plan was termed. Originally, troops were to be landed along a broad front from Ramsgate to the Isle of Wight, with a further three divisions landing around Bridport[1]. Naval concerns about the difficulty of

8

gaining sea control led to the abandonment of landings west of Brighton. This still provided scope for German armour to sweep south of London, to cross the middle Thames and cut off the capital. Churchill had declared his willingness to fight in the ruins of Whitehall. German recognition of the importance of London is shown by the study devoting one of its portfolios to the city, but the German army will not have relished the prospect of fighting for it street by street: the siege of Paris in 1871 is a precedent they probably had in mind, when artillery fire from around the city (together with starvation) had been sufficient to subdue the inhabitants. It is significant that the four 1:20 000 maps of London were the only ones in the initial study to be overprinted with the German artillery grid – a prerequisite for indirect fire.

In the event, Operation Sea Lion was postponed, initially to mid September. Then, when the *Luftwaffe* had patently failed to gain air superiority, it was deferred until at least the following year. The military geographers continued with their work, producing new editions of their study – the one used here dates from August 1941. The collection of photographs of 'military objects' and their marking on maps extended from 1941 to 1942. Meanwhile, the coastal views in Portfolio C were extended up the east coast as far as Perth and up the west coast to Oban.

The idea of collecting details of objects of military importance was fundamentally sound. We have already seen the importance of the river crossings of the Thames. The aerial view of Abingdon (PLATE 28) would be extremely useful to a commander planning how he could secure the bridge and causeway there, or dislodge an enemy from it. But the principle that bridges were 'military objects' was extended to include suburban railway bridges (PLATE 23) or the old Waterloo Bridge (PLATE 11) – even though its replacement was also illustrated, complete with engineering drawings.

Likewise, one can understand the interest of an army in flour mills (PLATE 15) or in vehicle repair facilities (PLATE 25) but it is difficult to see the military significance of a gramophone factory (PLATE 32). A military bureaucracy could be as self-perpetuating as any other sort of bureaucracy, especially when the consequence of disestablishment was likely to be service with the infantry on the Eastern Front.

At this point it is useful to consider the sources used by the Germans and the quality of their product. The compilers were not part of the Army Intelligence staffs. They tried to employ academics who had spent time in the subject country but there is no indication that anyone was ever sent to England to photograph 'military objects'. Nor were aerial photographs by the *Luftwaffe* employed. The *Luftwaffe* produced its own entirely separate geographical studies and its own compilation of targets for bombing. The photographs in the Army study here seem in general to have been culled from the libraries of Berlin; the maps are mostly based on Ordnance Survey material enlarged or reduced to a standard military scale.

One consequence of the sources used was that information was liable to be out of date. For example, the 'military object' photographs include a number of the timber railway viaducts which Brunel developed and of which all but one had gone by 1939. More seriously, the text includes a table of road surfaces by county, which is probably derived from highway engineers' reports for such counties and such dates as could be found. The German army was accustomed to operations in areas where the minor roads were quite unsuited to heavy military traffic; indeed, minor roads in Germany itself still left a lot to be desired. In contrast, the UK probably had some of the best-surfaced minor roads in the world by 1939. The use of old data in the tables quite obscures this and led to some false conclusions in the military evaluations. Finally, there are a number of gratuitous errors, unsurprising for a compilation initially assembled with such speed. For example, the map at Figure 1 shows a windmill symbol for a flour mill on the Victoria Embankment. These had been gardens since at least 1890 and anyone looking for a flour mill – or a windmill – there would be disappointed.

Thankfully, Operation Sea Lion never took place and most of the copies of this military-geographic study – it is thought that some seven thousand copies were printed – remained in map stores, awaiting an order that never came. In June 1944, a cross-Channel amphibious operation was indeed launched, but that was Operation Overlord, the Allied return to northern France. That operation showed just how difficult an opposed amphibious landing could be, even with complete air superiority and control of the sea. After the eventual breakthrough in France, Allied forces streamed eastwards and over-ran several of the German map stores. Copies of the unissued geographic studies were brought back to the UK and after the war were distributed to the major copyright libraries, including the Bodleian copy reproduced here. We hope this translation will be of value, whether for counter-factual historians considering the chances of success of a German invasion, for those interested in the state of England in 1939 as seen through German eyes, or simply for those pondering our merciful deliverance from the horrors of Nazi occupation.

Rob Wheeler

1 Führer Directive, 16 July 1940.
2 Ronald Wheatley, *Operation Sea Lion* (Oxford, 1958).

Editor's Note:

The text for this edition has been abridged and some of the headings have been altered. A few obvious typographical errors have also been corrected as well as some inconsistencies of style.

PART 1
Great Britain: Analysis and Vital Statistics

INTRODUCTION TO GREAT BRITAIN

1. Location, Size, Borders, Distances

In geographical terms, England is the main country in the British Isles; in political terms, it is the heartland of the United Kingdom of Great Britain and Northern Ireland.

It includes that part of the group of islands which faces the Continent. Its south-eastern point (Dover) is separated from northern France by the Pas de Calais, which is only 32 kilometres wide at its narrowest point. On average, the south coast is only 120 kilometres distant from its counterpart on the opposite side of the Channel in northern France. The east coast faces the North Sea; it is separated from the Dutch coast by 200 kilometres and from southern Norway by 560 kilometres. To the north, England is bordered by Scotland; they form a single geographical entity and are joined in real and personal union.

In the west, southern England meets the Atlantic Ocean, which gradually narrows and penetrates far inland along the Bristol Channel. Central and northern England, on the other hand, are bounded on this side by the landlocked Irish Sea. It is 200 kilometres wide, and the Isle of Man marks the halfway point. The northern approach to the Irish Sea, the North Channel, is only 35 kilometres wide, whereas the St George's Channel in the south has a width of 75 to 140 kilometres.

The significance of the location of England/the British Isles follows from the fact that they represent the western boundary of the North Sea.

Unlike Scotland, there are few islands in the waters surrounding England. There are none at all of any significance along the east coast, which is much smoother as a whole. The Isle of Wight nestles against the south coast, whereas the British Channel Islands, Alderney, Guernsey, and Jersey, are much closer to the French mainland. In the west, only the narrow Menai Strait separates Anglesey from north-west Wales, the Isle of Man is to be found in the middle of the Irish Sea, and the outlying Isles of Scilly are around 45 kilometres from the south-west tip of England.

The rise and fall of the tides varies enormously in timing and magnitude around the English coast. When England's west coast is experiencing high tide, it is low tide on the east coast. Particularly high tidal ranges occur in the bays that cut far back into the coastline.

The main island is 900 kilometres in length from north to south; of this, England makes up 600 kilometres. The width of the island from east to west is at its greatest, 460 kilometres, on the south coast; in the middle it is around 400 kilometres; and in northern England it is only 150 kilometres. A number of bays, moreover, cut far back into the coastline and considerably reduce the width of the island still further in several places: the Thames estuary (60 kilometres long) and the Wash (40 kilometres long) in the east, for example, and the Bristol Channel (160 kilometres), Morecambe Bay (30 kilometres), and the Solway Firth (60 kilometres) in the west.

TABLE OF DISTANCES

Some **distances**		In comparison	
London-Edinburgh (Scotland)	460km	Berlin-Essen	460km
London-Dublin (Ireland)	430km	Berlin-Frankfurt am Main	425km
London-Dover	100km	Berlin-Cottbus	100km
London-Paris	350km	Berlin-Nuremberg	370km
London-Brussels	310km	Berlin-Breslau	290km
London-Manchester	260km	Berlin-Hamburg	255km
London-Brighton	75km	Berlin-Frankfurt an der Oder	80km

2. The State

Together with Scotland, Northern Ireland, and the Channel Islands, England forms a single state: the United Kingdom of Great Britain and Northern Ireland.

1931	Area, km²	Inhabitants	Population density
England and Wales	151,105	39,952,380	264
Scotland	77,168	4,842,980	63
Northern Ireland	14,136	1,279,750	91
Isle of Man & Channel Islands	766	142,510	185

The **system of government** is that of a constitutional monarchy. Legislative authority lies with Parliament, which consists of two houses, the upper house (House of Lords) and lower house (House of Commons). Executive authority lies nominally with the Crown, but is held by the cabinet of ministers in practice.

The state is divided into **administrative divisions** called *counties* and *county boroughs* (i.e. urban areas given the same status as counties), which have fairly extensive autonomy. These powers are exercised by the county councils (sheriff, justices of the peace, and other officials), and cover highways, economic development, general welfare, education, and so on.

The counties are subdivided into *county districts*, either rural or urban, which themselves have autonomous administrative bodies and responsibilities.

A number of towns, some of which are county boroughs and some of which are not, have the status of autonomous *municipal corporations* with mayor, aldermen, and burgesses, as well a town council to act as administrative body.

WEATHER AND CLIMATE

The English climate is characterized by a high level of humidity, heavy cloud cover, considerable amounts of precipitation, modest warmth in summer, and mild temperatures in winter.

England receives on average only a third of the possible amount of **sunshine**. The other two thirds are lost to cloud and mist, and winter in particular is distinguished by its lack of sunlight. Consequently, **precipitation** is unusually common in England, albeit somewhat less so the further one moves away from the western hills and coastline towards the south-eastern part of the country.

MINING AND INDUSTRY AND THE URBAN SETTLEMENTS; ENERGY SUPPLY

(See the map of England's industrial areas at the end of this book)

Despite its many agrarian areas, England as a whole is a great accumulation of factories and attendant residential settlements, which have been built and expanded to an extent that far exceeds what the land is naturally able to support. In terms of area alone, these industrialized urban settlements occupy a considerable part of the island; the imbalance is increased still further by the continued decline in the population and settlements of large tracts of land.

The structure of the English industrial system is complex; the underlying foundation is provided by the mining industry, whose output is about the same in value as that of the agricultural sector if the latter's internal consumption is ignored. **Coal** makes up 88 per cent of mining output (200 to 250 million tonnes per year). England has enormous coal reserves in the form of numerous coalfields adjoining the edges of the mountain massifs.

English coal-mining is characterized by the presence of a large number of relatively small mining operations. Because of this and the general principle of obtaining the greatest output or greatest profit at the least expense, industrial practices and extraction methods are to a large extent outdated and insufficiently mechanized and rationalized; as a result, they have ceased to be capable of achieving maximum productivity. Only during the post-war period were successful measures taken in pursuit of improvement, consolidation, and more substantial mechanization.

The mining of ore, above all iron ore, is widespread; it is now of less importance, but certainly still capable of expansion. Deposits of ore occur near both the old rocks of the mountains and the more recent strata of the eastern lowlands, in accumulations similar to those formed by minette in Lorraine.

The major centres of heavy industry, which almost everywhere developed with the help of coal, are now to be found in the industrial region of north-east England, in south Wales, and in central England. A shift towards the coast has begun to take place more recently as the use of ore from outside becomes ever more widespread.

Heavy industry provides the foundation for shipbuilding and ship repair on the one hand (north-east coast of England; Birkenhead, near Liverpool; Barrow (Cumberland); Devonport; Chatham (Thames); Portsmouth; Southampton), and ironmongery and mechanical industry on the other (particularly widespread in central England, but also present in most other towns and cities). The situation is similar with respect to vehicle manufacture. The textile industry, too, has become concentrated around the coalfields: cotton processing has its focus primarily in the industrial area of Lancashire, west of the Pennines; wool processing in the Leeds–Bradford area, east of the Pennines; knitwear and other branches of the textile industry in the area south of the Pennines, and in the rest of central England. The north-west part of central England is also home to the older chemical industry and the ceramics industry.

These older industries have declined since the World War and are generally ailing. The new industries (modern chemical, rubber, car, electrical, and armament industries of all kinds, as well as the consumer goods industry) are largely dependent on electric power alone; they have a tendency to establish themselves not only in the old industrial regions of the north, but also in central and southern England. Significant new factories have developed in a favourable market here.

Most of England's industrial settlements grew up a long time ago, when no one thought about town planning. Residential housing and factories of all kinds are therefore to be found right next to one another. In many cases, a tangled clutter has developed, posing considerable difficulties where contemporary standards of hygiene and the demands of modern transport are concerned. Furthermore, the condition of the buildings in most old areas of workers' housing has gradually reached such a catastrophic state that hardly any of the old industrial towns have been spared the 'slum problem'. By this is meant the problem of providing new, humane housing for many tens of thousands of people, while at the same time separating industrial and residential quarters and creating an adequate transport network. English industrial towns are typified by the cloud of smoke that is constantly lying over them; it is the cause of the thick fog that appears in foggy weather. England's working-class quarters contain lines of identical houses that could not be smaller and in many cases have no yards or gardens, with the result that the towns spread out over a considerable area. The residential districts and suburbs of the larger towns extend far out into the surrounding countryside. Single-family homes are predominant. The dense rail and road network with bus transport allows people to inhabit a considerable area and the urban population to spread into the countryside as described above.

Energy Supply

The most important sources of power in England are linked together in an energy ring by the Central Electricity Board. Electricity is generated at a common frequency in the major power stations and transmitted to the distributing substations along the main electricity supply lines (known as the grid).

There are 137 major power stations (beginning of 1939) with a combined output of 8,264.1 million watts. The largest of them is the County of London Electric Supply Company's power station in Barking (462.5 million watts); other major power stations are designed to produce 200 to 350 million watts. The construction of two new power stations is planned: by the Thames in south-east England at Littlebrook, and at Little Barford. There are 304 distributing power stations, transformation stations, and switching stations (known as grid points). The biggest transformation station is to be found at Barking, which has four transformers with a capacity of 60 million volt amperes each and six with a capacity of 30 million volt amperes each; there are two 75 million volt ampere transformers at Clarence Dock power station in Liverpool. The biggest transformation station in terms of area and number of switches is that at Northfleet in south-east England. The cost of constructing the grid system had amounted to almost 30 million pounds by the end of 1936.

Electricity generation and distribution is directed by seven load-dispatching centres (the largest is in Bankside, London). A dedicated telephone network with over 10,000 kilometres of cabling is used to help manage the grid system.

Power company	Power stations	Voltage (kV)	Connected load (MW)	Generator output	No. of substations	Supplies
Clyde Valley Electrical Power Co. and Associated	Yoker Clydes Mill Stonebyres }Wasser Bonnington]	11	100 68			shipyards, steelworks, coalmines companies
Cornwall Electric Power Co.	Hayle	11 33	96	17.8	500	14 major industrial consumers
Derbyshire & Nottinghamshire Electric Power Co.	Spondon	11 33 66	238	124	954	
Fife Electric Power Co.	Townhill, Dunfermline	3 6.6 12 20 33	65	19.5	510	
Kent Electric Power Co.	Littlebrook, nr. Dartford, under construction			85		4 major industrial consumers
Lancashire Electric Power Co. Kearsley	Ringley Road, Padiham,	33	194	58.5 30.6 162.25	639	
Leicestershire & Warwickshire Electric Power Co.	Hinckley Warwick	6.6 11 12 33	152	8 18	666	
Metropolitan	—	—	199	—	29 4 transformers, 25 rectifiers	low-voltage distribution in London, managed by London Power Co.
Midland Electric Corporation For Power Distribution	—	27	189 7	—	55	8 major consumers and West Midlands Joint Electricity Authority
North-Eastern Electric Supply Co. Ltd.	Carville Dunston A North Tees Dunston B	6 11 20	1,000	62.5 30 110 200	1,680	London North East. Railway coalmines, furnaces, dockyards, factories.
North Metropolitan Electric Power Supply Co.	Brimsdown B Willesden, currently being rebuilt. Brimsdown A	3 10.5 22 33		107.5 — 53	1,039	

Power company	Power stations	Voltage (kV)	Connected load (MW)	Generator output	No. of substations	Supplies
North Wales Power Co. Ltd.	Maentwrog} Hydro-electric Cwm Dyli power Dolgar-rog stations	6,6 11 20 33	78	58.75	236	mines and steelworks, railways
Shropshire, Worcestershire and Staffordshire Electric Power Co.	Stourport ? Hereford	3.3 5.5 11 33 66	457	86 (+ 60 under construction) ? 4		various factories and railways
Scottish Central Electric Power Co.	Bonnybridge	3 6 20	18.2	22.25	185	
South Wales Electric Power Co.	Upper Boat	11 33	209	123	608	many large coal-mines, steelworks and tin mining/ processing works, shipyards, railways
West Kent Electric Co. Ltd. North-West Kent	–	–	90	–	–	
Yorkshire Electric Power Co.	Thornhill Barugh Ferrybridge	11 33 66	321	64.5 14 40	1,275	

TRANSPORT

England is one of the most mobile countries in the world. The natural conditions for the development of a transport network are very good: the greater part of the country is relatively flat, and even the mountainous parts, in Wales and Scotland, can be crossed easily with the help of the valleys and low-lying passes.

England has a dense and well-developed road network, a rail network with excellent coverage, a canal system that was effective when first created, and a thriving coastal shipping sector.

The figures for goods transport give the best overview of how the various modes of transport within Great Britain compare. The loads carried in 1937 were as follows:

by train. . . . . 300,000,000 tonnes (63.3%)

by HGV (i.e. on the roads) . . . . 140,000,000 tonnes (31.3%)

by canal . . . . 24,700,000 tonnes (5.4%)

Coastal shipping carried 55 to 60 million tonnes, which was about a fifth of that transported by rail.

The railways are therefore the spine of England's internal transportation system; HGV traffic constitutes a third of the total, but is significant only in carrying goods a short distance at the beginning and end of a journey. Road transport is therefore of little importance as a way of relieving the burden on the rail network if the latter is affected by delays or disruption.

1. Roads

General

The total length of the British road network (England, Wales, and Scotland) is approximately 287,000 kilometres. Of this, 66,080 kilometres consist of streets and roads in urban areas and 220,160 kilometres of roads elsewhere. Comparison of the English road network with that of Germany yields the following figures:

For every 100 km² there are

120 km of road in England

60 km of road in Germany (the Reich prior to 1938). England can therefore be described as a country with very many roads. It may well be the country with the most roads in the world in proportion to its size. These average statistics, however, must not be taken to mean that England possesses a road network of uniform coverage. Instead, traffic density is concentrated in a number of areas.

London must be mentioned first and foremost in this respect. Twenty million people live in the area bounded by Harwich, Oxford, Southampton, and Dover alone, and here the road network is extremely dense and comprehensive in its coverage. London is the hub from which all roads radiate outwards.

A second area in which the densest traffic will be found is the Liverpool, Leeds, and Birmingham triangle; here alone, there are a further 10 million inhabitants. Two thirds of the English people are packed into these two areas, and the coverage of the road network is accordingly comprehensive within them.

In the north, the area between Glasgow and Edinburgh is, with its 3.2 million people, another area with a remarkably dense road network. Otherwise, there is a marked tendency for roads to run towards the coast, where a large number of important towns are to be found.

Other areas, above all Wales, northern England, and all of Scotland apart from the Glasgow–Edinburgh area, however, have far fewer roads.

On the whole, the roads meet the considerable demands placed on them by civilian traffic. The road network is not exemplary, but the roads are numerous and kept in good condition; there are excellent links between the ports and the main industrial areas, and much is done in maintaining the road network to ensure it remains at its current level.

Above all, the condition of England's long-distance roads is generally excellent. (See PLATES 4 AND 13)

England's long-distance road network consists of trunk roads — a relatively small network of main roads with a length of 4,500 English miles (7,200 kilometres) that has been under the direct control of the British Department of Transport since 1 April 1937.

Classification of English Roads; Road Management

According to the most recent data available, the following figures are indicative of the division and length of the network:

Class A roads . . . . 22,600 English miles
(around 36,000 kilometres)

Class B roads . . . . 16,900 English miles
(around 27,100 kilometres)

unclassified roads
(local roads, country roads) . . . . . . 134,832 English miles
(around 215,730 kilometres)

Class A roads are main roads. Class B roads are generally roads that connect smaller towns. The non-classified roads (scheduled roads) include those roads with small amounts of traffic and those whose condition is not sufficient to meet the prescribed requirements for classified roads. Responsibility for classes A and B lies with the county councils. Road maintenance is good.

Since the new law on road-building was passed, only 10 to 12 per cent of the overall funding for road-building has been assigned to the **construction of new roads**, which is understandable given the size of the network as it is. Most of the budget is allocated instead to improving existing roads and their bridges, as well as to ongoing maintenance and upkeep, which have together claimed 75 per cent of the total funds.

Road Construction

English road-building plans have long been dominated by economic considerations regarding road construction and usage. Consequently, importance is attached to

Plate 1 (Canal) *Typical canal scene in Hertfordshire.*
Towpath along the Grand Junction Canal near Boxmoor, west of St Albans.

Plate 2 (Windsor Castle) Aerial photograph of Windsor Castle.
The royal castle is on a rocky spur some 50 metres high above the Thames (far bottom right); behind it the park. Two stations, bottom left and centre right.

Plate 3 (Bristol, bridge) *Suspension bridge above the entrance to Bristol Harbour.*
Looking downstream from the City Docks towards the channel for sea-going ships.
The bridge is 412 metres in length and 87 metres above the low-water mark.

Plate 4 (Sussex road) *Modern main road in Sussex. Brighton Road, near Pycombe.*

Plate 5 (Canterbury from the air) Aerial photograph of Canterbury in the *Stour valley.* The famous cathedral is in the foreground, seen here from the south looking towards the Thames estuary.

Plate 6 (Canal, frozen) Grand Junction Canal near Sudbury, west of London.

Plate 7 (Coventry) Coventry: *Road-building in progress.*
The layout of industrial towns in the Midlands is generally crowded and confusing.
The view here is of the western part of the city centre, seen from the south-east.

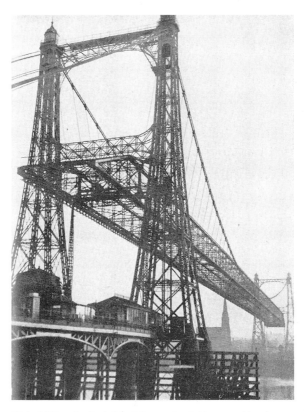

Plate 8 (Manchester bridge) *Suspension bridge near Manchester.*
Raising suspension bridge over the Mersey and Manchester Canal at
Runcorn–Widnes at the eastern end of the Mersey bay.

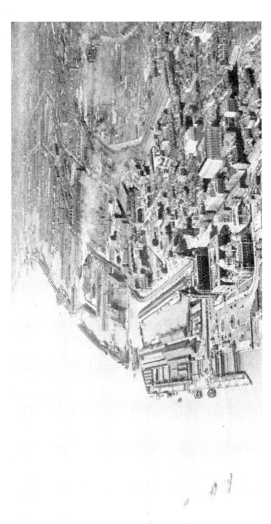

Plate 9 (Liverpool) *Liverpool city and harbour.*

The Mersey is on the left; the docks and port basins run from south to north along its right-hand bank. Terminals for passenger steamers can be seen in the foreground. The city of Liverpool is on the right. View downstream from the south-east, looking towards the northern part of the docks.

Plate 10 (Blackfriars Bridge) *View of Blackfriars Bridge.*

The railway bridge leading to Blackfriars station is on the right. Behind, St Paul's Cathedral. View of the City (left bank).

Plate 11 (Old Waterloo Bridge) *Old Waterloo Bridge and replacement bridge.* The new bridge has since been completed. View of the City (left bank).

Plate 12 (Hammersmith Bridge)

Plate 13 (Malden motorway) *'Motorway' at Malden.*

The Kingston Bypass Road in south-west London, sometimes with footbridges. Left-hand traffic!

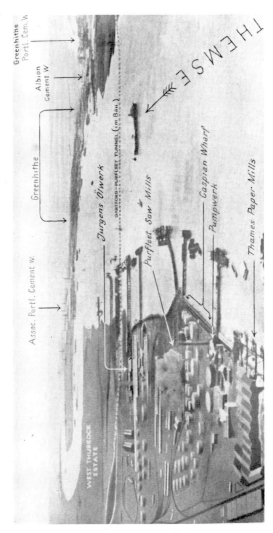

Plate 14 (Thames) *Industrial complex on the Thames, north of Dartford.*

Left: paper mills, pumping station, docks, sawmills, oil plant. Right: Greenhithe and Albion cement works, and Portland cement works complex. Looking downstream. [In the picture: Pumpwerk > Pumping station, Themes > Thames, im Bau > under construction, Jurgens Ölwerk > Jurgen oil plant]

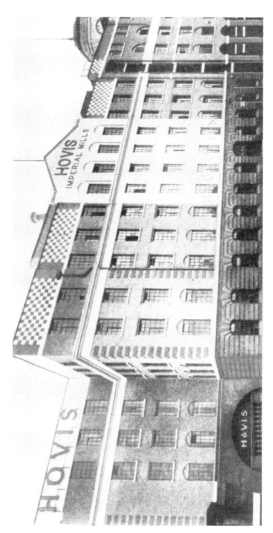

Plate 15 (Hovis) *Major Hovis mill, Westminster.*

Plate 16 (Battersea) *Battersea Power Station on the south bank of the Thames.*
On the right is Grosvenor Bridge (rail), behind it the new Chelsea Bridge and Battersea Park. Looking upstream.

Plate 17 (Westminster) Westminster Bridge with the Houses of Parliament (Westminster Palace) above the bridge on the north bank.

Plate 18 (The City) *The City of London.*
The Stock Exchange is the building with columns in the centre. The Bank of England is to the left of it. Victoria Street is in the foreground. The streets are generally narrow, busy, and angular.

Plate 19 (Tower Bridge) *Aerial photograph of the inner London docks.*

Tower Bridge is in the foreground, the great warehouses and ancient dockyards of the Port of London in the background: London Docks, and in front of them the oldest of them all, St Catherine's Docks.

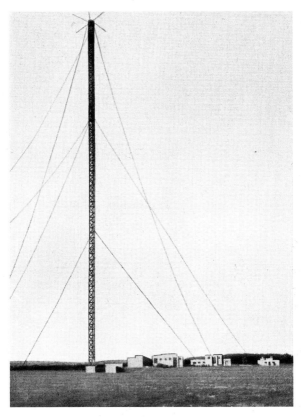

Plate 20 (BBC mast) *British Broadcasting Corporation transmission point at Stagshaw, near Newcastle-upon-Tyne.* Iron mast, 148 metres high, with capacity ring. Operates at 60 kW.

Plate 21 (Tyne road bridge) *New road bridge over the Tyne in Newcastle-upon-Tyne (Northumberland).* Iron road bridge across the river Tyne. Compressed trussed arch of constant strength; the tie bar serves as carriageway. Span: 175 metres. In the background is the rail bridge of the London and North Eastern Railway (pillars supporting tracks).

Plate 22 (ICI) *Oil storage unit of Imperial Chemical Industries in Billingham.* Oil tanks for the coal hydrogenation plant at Billingham Reach oil pier (river Tees).

Plate 23 (Tolworth station) *Railway bridge at Tolworth station (south-west London).*
This concrete rail bridge over the Kingston–Ewell road lies on Southern Railway's line between Wimbledon and Weybridge. It was built in 1938 and intended to have two roads pass underneath it. Beam: length of 31 metres, weight of 58 tonnes.

Plate 24 (Knaresborough) *Road bridge in Knaresborough (Yorkshire, West Riding).*
Stone bridge over the river Nidd on the road from Harrogate to Knaresborough.

Compressed semicircular arches with small turrets support the carriageway. The arch on the right-hand side of the bridge allows a road to pass underneath. The town with its castle is on the hillside to the right.

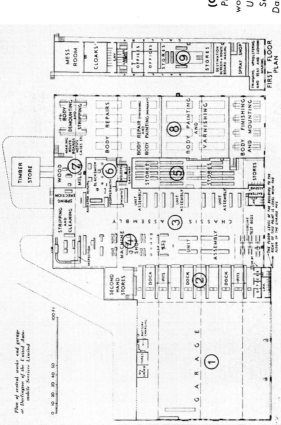

Plate 25
(Cars, Darlington)
Plan of the central
works and garage of
United Automobile
Services Limited at
Darlington (Durham).

Plate 26 (Conway bridge) *Road bridge in Conway (Caernarvonshire).*
View of the suspension bridge (built in 1826) from Conway Castle. Suspension cables strung between massive walled pylons with ramparts. Behind, half-hidden, is the railway bridge.

Plate 27 (Power station) *Kirkstall Power Station, near Leeds (Yorkshire).*

New electric power station. Voltage: 26,611 kV; maximum load: 116,440 kW; generator: 147,000 kW (total output).

Plate 28 (Abingdon)

Road bridge over the Thames at Abingdon (Berkshire).

Arched stone bridge over the Thames on the road from Culham to Abingdon.

POWER HOUS.

SINTER PLANT

COAL & COAL HANDLING PLANT

ORE YARD

COKE OVEN PLANT

BLAST FURNACE

DRY QUENCHING PLANT

PIG CASTING MACHINE

HOT METAL BUILDING

BY PRODUCTS PLANT

ELECTRIC UNLOADERS

FOUNDRY

ADMINISTRATION BUILDING

PIG IRON STORE YARD

MANUFACTURING & ASSEMBLY SHOPS

CAR DESPATCH

Plate 29 (Ford factory) *Ford Car Factory on the Thames at Dagenham (Essex).*

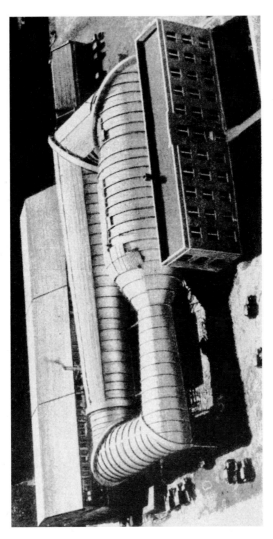

Plate 30 (Farnborough) *Aircraft construction research unit in Farnborough (Hampshire).* The wind tunnel is located between the two buildings.

Plate 31 (Grand Union Canal)

The canal is shown here crossing the North Circular Road near Wembley, north-west London.

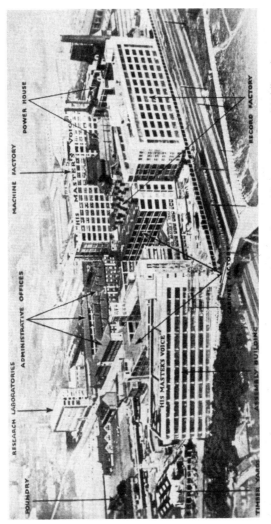

Plate 32 (HMV) *His Master's Voice: gramophone and record factory in Hayes (Middlesex).*

good, strong foundations, and care is taken to ensure that surfaces are carefully maintained and kept in good condition. The current road network is dense and extensive and therefore presents considerable difficulties where the construction of significant new roads, in particular of a new road network, is concerned. Thus, in the last fifteen years, hardly any new major roads creating truly new links have been built, apart from the construction of 400 kilometres of major roads in the area around London and the rebuilding of the Birmingham–Wolverhampton, Glasgow–Edinburgh, and Liverpool–East Lancashire roads. In the last seven years, around 450 kilometres of bypasses and side roads in urban areas have been created (see PLATE 13). On the other hand, much has been done to improve the existing road network: the addition of more appropriate surfaces has been widely funded so as to improve the capacity of existing roads and adapt them as much as possible to the demands made by increasing quantities of traffic. In addition to the improvement of road surfaces, bridges have been built, subgrades widened, excessively sharp bends removed, markings applied, and so on. The **motorway question** is thus approached in a different context in England than it is in other countries. The density of the existing road network, together with the use of the countryside for building as well as agricultural purposes, inevitably places constraints on the siting of independent, direct motorways for the use of road traffic alone. Motorways of this nature are therefore not currently to be found (see PLATE 13).

Typical roads, including those of class A and B, and in particular the unclassified roads, have an average width of 20 feet (i.e. 6 metres), have frequent bends, and are, particularly in southern and central England, lined by the ubiquitous hedges, which are not particularly helpful for vehicle traffic. Even so, work to improve and widen these roads, and even add a second lane if demand requires it, has been underway continuously for twenty years. The new roads to have been built have generally been larger or smaller arterial roads, sometimes leading to the nearest major traffic hub, sometimes connecting existing main roads. The building of **roads around built-up areas** has emerged as a novel means of reducing the pressures of modern vehicle traffic. The design of these bypasses, as they are known, can be seen as exemplary, even if the execution does not match the high standard set by the motorways of the Reich. (See PLATE 13)

If the course of the older English roads is winding, seldom straight, and dictated by local conditions, it is clear that considerable attention has been paid to the needs of vehicle traffic in the planning and execution of work on the road network during the last twenty years. The desired speed of travel is high, so planners aim to achieve a course that is direct, has as large a radius of curvature as possible, and passes over or under railways where level crossings can be avoided. Cuttings of around 20 metres in depth and embankments of almost 17 metres in height are therefore to be found along new roads of this kind (Watling Street).

Surfacing Material

In England, like almost everywhere else, the composition of a road's surface depends on the materials available on the spot. In Great Britain, road metal or **hard stone** is usual in the macadam layer, and a layer of hard stone as the foundation for roads. Today, the material is bound with the modern binding agents of **tar, asphalt** in various forms, and **cement**. In addition to these roads with a rock component, there are also those with a wooden surface, which were introduced as long ago as the time when wagons were drawn by iron-shod horses. This surface has indeed disappeared from the main routes, but it will still be encountered on roads in residential parts of the towns. Sand and gravel are obtained from the coastline and the rivers. Limestone is the predominant type of rock available for use; almost eight million tonnes of it are broken up and used for road-building purposes annually; basalt, too, is a popular choice. **Limestone** is present throughout the south-east, from Dover to Dorchester on the English Channel and Harborough on the North Sea. The limestone is joined by Jurassic rock from Cleveland to Dorchester/Portland (a peninsula extending into the Channel from southern England whose famous limestone has been used for road-building since 1830). The Jurassic rock also extends along a broad front from south-west to north-east. Next comes sandstone, and finally the coal region, which provides the **tar** that has been extensively used in road-building in England for a long time. It has been joined by **asphalt**, which was imported from the colonies and entered use in a variety of forms in England, as elsewhere.

Types of Surface

The following are the main kinds of surface to have appeared, as a result of the raw materials available, in England:

1. tarmacadam surface,
2. various kinds of asphalt surface, in particular rolled asphalt,
3. concrete surface,
4. stone paving surfaces (large and small blocks),
5. wooden surface,
6. water-bound macadam surface,
7. gravel surface produced by treatment of the top layer.

If a **rough impression of how frequent these types of surface are** is desired, the following approximations can be suggested:

1. tarmacadam surfaces . . . . around 50–55%
2. rolled asphalt surfaces . . . . around 30–33%
3. concrete surfaces . . . . around 6–8%
4. all other types of surface mentioned . . . . around 8–10%

The figures, rough as they may be, show if nothing else how important roads made with tar are in England. **Thus, if the asphalt surfaces are included, approximately 85 per cent of all surfaces are blacktop**; the percentage is probably even greater if colour is taken as a guide, for there has been a move in places to add a coating of tar to concrete roads as well, increasing their resistance to wear and tear in the process. Tar and bitumen consumption corresponds to the figures regarding construction given above; in 1938, 900,000 tonnes of tar and 480,000 to 500,000 tonnes of asphalt and bitumen were used. Use of concrete is constantly increasing, not only for purely concrete surfaces, but also, in particular, because a concrete layer is being included more and more frequently in other kinds of road being built.

Road Traffic and Motorization

England's major traffic is concentrated along some 20,000 kilometres of roadway: the main roads of the major towns on the one hand, the long-distance routes (arterial roads and bypasses) on the other. The primary factors responsible for this traffic are the two main centres with enormous concentrations of people described above: Greater London and its wider surroundings with over 20 million people, and the industrial triangle of Liverpool, Leeds, and Birmingham in central England with over 10 million people. These two important centres, with both their own internal traffic and that between them, are the main contributors to traffic volume. The area around the two centres, extending across nearly 300 kilometres, subsumes almost half of all freight and passenger traffic in England. The challenge posed by this traffic is met by around eighteen major railway lines and the existing road network. On the latter, motor buses join lorries and private cars and help to ensure an orderly flow of traffic.

Traffic is also assisted by the special measures that have been taken at **road junctions** in England, in particular on the large arterial roads of the big towns, especially London.

Great importance is also attached to the provision of **traffic signs** on the open road: warning signs for drivers (e.g. indicating crossings, as in 'next crossing 50 yards'); crossing signs for pedestrians; warnings of merging main roads; and the recent practice of painting large printed directions such as 'Danger', 'look right', or 'cross here' on the roads themselves. Such devices are the expression of an often primitive but nonetheless effective concern for marking danger-spots and ensuring that traffic flow reflects the interests of road users. **Signposts and direction indicators** including place names are to be found everywhere in normal times. According to press reports, however, they have already been removed due to fear of the 'invasion' at the present time. **Cycle tracks** are planned, but construction has so far been limited. At the beginning of 1939, only 500 miles or so (around 800 kilometres) of them had been built in the whole of England.

Finally, mention should be made of the telephone system on the main roads. It must operate well in normal times: the siting of telephone boxes at regular intervals allows any desired telephone connection to be made without leaving the road. It remains to be seen how accessible this facility would be if things became serious.

A dense network of **petrol stations**, each of which has four to eight pumps, is designed to supply drivers with fuel.

Road Bridges

The strength of English road bridges is high. There are load regulations for individual cases, but they are very complicated and of little value when it comes to practical use.

The road networks of the individual English counties (In miles*), broken down according to road class and surface material

County	Size of administrative area in square miles	A class roads (trunk roads)	B class roads	Unclassified roads	Total	Wooden surface	Stone paving (granite and others)	Asphalt	Concrete	Tarmacadam	Water-bound surface	Surface of inferior quality	Thin surface of tar or bitumen
Anglesey	276.0	81.40	68.46	554.00	707.45	·	·	·	·	50.00		·	650.00
Bedfordshire	473.5	99.92	68.41	597.32	819.94					248.30	571.64	·	807.26
Berkshire	710.0	239.26 / 58.56	169.36	1,058.12	1,525.30								
Breconshire	733.0	154.00	65.00	955.00	1174.00	·	·	·	1.08	95.00	507.00	571.00	353.00
Buckinghamshire	264.09	165.77	1,197.55	1,627.61	1.00	.37	100.04	20.20	268.00	1,105.00	113.00	1,350.00	
Caernarvonshire	56.9	110.81 / 38.05	120.14	816.12	1,085.12	·	·	3.0	1.25	60.00	992.14	40.00	992.14
Cambridgeshire	490.0	129.32 / 17.04	99.49	547.15	793.00								
Cardiganshire	700.0	164.65	205.20	971.19	1,341.04								
Carmarthenshire	947.0	150.98 / 67.48	110.91	1,788.52	2,050.41								
Cheshire	973.0	434.0 / 85.0	1,387.0	2,159.0									
Cornwall	1,334.0	355.0 / 76.0	352.0	3,070.0	3,853.0								
Cumberland	1,513.4	225.05 / 48.0	252.59	1,810.94	2,336.58								
Debighshire	1,008.0	344.22	266.14	1,596.15	2,293.45								
Derbyshire		86.94											
Devon (N.W.Division)													
Devon (S.E.Division)		317.50 / 86.20	237.10	3,078.60	3,719.40								

The road networks of the individual English counties (in miles*), broken down according to road class and surface material

County	Size of administrative area in square miles	A class roads (trunk roads)	B class roads	Unclassified roads	Total	Wooden surface	Stone paving (granite and others)	Asphalt	Concrete	Tarmacadam	Water-bound surface	Surface of inferior quality	Thin surface of tar or bitumen
Dorset		269.69 16.74	210.10	1,415.55	1,912.08	·	·	13.50	·	197.00	1,576.00	28.27	·
Durham													
Ely, Isle of		77.23	135.54 16.94	361.15	590.86	.50	.17	1.88	13.25	177.00	350.06		590.86
Essex	1,505.69	420.75	442.15 84.27	1,957.41	2,820.31	.70	·	1.72	2.73	295.33	320.90		530.95
Flintshire	255.70	116.97	71.84 30.15	482.02	700.98		·					71.54	
Glamorgan	733.00	242.21	188.40 22.34	814.15	1,267.10								
Gloucestershire	1222.88	350.59	313.57 89.43	2,211.77	2,965.37								
Hampshire (Southampton)	1,416.24	391.63	248.24 98.55	2,459.27	3,197.69	·	·	184.69	5.80	989.20	1,743.07	272.19	2,165.14
Herefordshire	525.16	272.70	176.82	1,394.15	1,843.67								
Hertfordshire	632.06	228.00	162.00 56.00	1,010.00	1,456.00								
Huntingdonshire	365.60	78.95	103.96 31.93	369.41	584.25	.50	.20	61.61	9.00	200.00	287.94	25.00	534.00
Kent	1,517.60	546.73	421.30 53.96	2,773.51	3,795.50	10.00	·	65.07	30.73	868.97	2321.39	142.19	2796.99
Lancashire	1,622.07	285.82	231.25 104.56	402.86	1,024.49								

The road networks of the individual English counties (in miles*), broken down according to road class and surface material

County	Size of administrative area in square miles	A class roads (trunk roads)	B class roads	Unclassified roads	Total	Wooden surface	Stone paving (granite and others)	Asphalt	Concrete	Tarmacadam	Water-bound surface	Surface of inferior quality	Thin surface of tar or bitumen
Leicestershire	806.00	168.01 / 54.89	205.18	1,200.41	1,573.60								
Lincolnshire, Holland	418.0	82.41 / 26.59	98.00	967.00	1,174.00								
Lincolnshire, Kesteven	724.0	134.08 / 21.39	138.02	1,241.36	1,534.85								
Lincolnshire, Lindsey	1,502.0	348.90 / 80.41	315.60	2,163.20	2,908.11		1.00	2.00	.50	361.00	732.00	732.00	1,069.00
London*	117.0	4.85	.40	.78	6.03	1.43	1.78	.87					1.43
Merioneth	659.9	167.13	72.95	667.40	907.48								
Middlesex	148.69	248.67	119.61	4.67	372.95								
Monmouthshire	531.42	151.86 / 46.31	99.56	862.31	1,160.04								
Montgomery	797.04	132.85 / 31.58	186.65	1,148.70	1,499.78					50.0	1,050.0	399.83	600.0
Norfolk		415.30 / 96.75	490.4	3,786.9	4,789.35			.60	1.5	1,457.90	2,903.35	426.0	3,263.80
Northampton	904.60	269.94 / 49.81	124.76	1,309.26	1,753.77		.18	41.79	3.78	563.96	872.83	271.23	1,499.44
Northumberland	1,998.67	300.32 / 102.66	363.72	1,060.61	2,827.31		2.42	14.72	4.50	1,381.60	1,279.74	135.57	1,393.84
Nottinghamshire													

The road networks of the individual English counties (in miles*), broken down according to road class and surface material

County	Size of administrative area in square miles	A class roads (trunk roads)	B class roads	Unclassified roads	Total	Wooden surface	Stone paving (granite and others)	Asphalt	Concrete	Tarmacadam	Water-bound surface	Surface of inferior quality	Thin surface of tar or bitumen
Oxfordshire	735.0	207.42 51.76	200.90	1,145.94	1,606.02			.16		124.50	1,351.57	57.10	729.74
Pembrokeshire	613.0	111.28 24.84	128.81	1,261.50	1,501.59	·	·		.26	58.92	88.68	3.62	96.75
Peterborough	83.5		15.75	112.63	153.22	·	·		2.0				
Radnorshire	470.57	76.07 24.92	84.11	837.45	1,022.55	·	·		.25	46.64	115.80	827.28	206.20
Rutland (Northern)		13.77 7.23	8.15	145.63	174.78								
Rutland (Southern)		15.59 13.97	11.44	89.45	130.45								
Salop	1,346.0	273.0 109.22	339.0	2,569.0	3,290.22	·	·						
Somerset	1,607.80	462.71 86.33	333.86	3,561.97	4444.87	·	·	31.51	1.71	1,160.02	2,919.46	200.98	3,727.27
Staffordshire													
Suffolk, East	870.86	141.36 56.64	299.63	1,410.06	1,907.69								
Suffolk, West	610.0	146.20 14.45	134.31	904.45	1,199.41								
Surrey	702.0	366.78 67.49	256.27	718.77	1,409.31								
Sussex, East	780.69	307.75 16.56	210.63	1,001.01	1,535.95	4.10	·	18.56	40.39	9.62	·	36.33	
Sussex, West	628.0	287.82 4.54	115.46	858.10	1,265.92								1,410.39

The road networks of the individual English counties (in miles*), broken down according to road class and surface material

County	Size of administrative area in square miles	A class roads (trunk roads)	B class roads	Unclassified roads	Total	Wooden surface	Stone paving (granite and others)	Asphalt	Concrete	Tarmacadam	Water-bound surface	Surface of inferior quality	Thin surface of tar or bitumen
Warwickshire	-	214.53 87.09	237.17	1,190.64	1,729.43								
Westmorland	789.0	124.02 61.81	89.78	791.55	1,067.16				1.00	201.20	664.70	200.26	580.76
Wight, Isle of	150.0	76.21	31.65	447.20	555.06				4.00	250.0	250.0	50.0	350.0
Wiltshire	1,345.0	357.16 51.22	176.77	2,166.63	2,751.78			37.60	3.33a	705.43	1,582.72	294.71	1,874.20
Worcestershire	-	278.40 28.81	206.80	1,310.50	1,824.51								
Yorkshire, East Riding	1,151.0	261.97	227.12	1,717.25	2,206.35			11.25	6.58	496.86	1,533.68	157.98	1315.16
Yorkshire, North-Riding	2,120.0	362.03 56.33	230.29	2,414.14	3,062.79								
Yorkshire, West Riding	2,517.0	764.18 157.53	491.50	2620.43	4033.64	.11	33.34	64.52	8.25	2,195.62	153.56	1,436.10	3,183.64

*1 English mile = 1.609 kilometres.

2. Railways

Development of the rail network has benefited from highly favourable environmental conditions on the island. England, the oldest railway country in the world, has a very tightly knit network with a density relative to surface area that is bettered only by Belgium.

The length of the railway network of Great Britain and Northern Ireland is 32,300 kilometres.

There is therefore 1 kilometre of track for every 7.5 square kilometres.

The density of the English rail network is thus 25 per cent greater than that of the German one.

Organization. Unlike in Germany, the railways of England are run by private companies, grouped together as follows since the post-war period:

1. The London, Midland and Scottish Railway (L.M.S.R.), with a track length of . . . . 11,166 km
2. London and North Eastern Railway (L.N.E.R.), with a track length of . . . . 10,265 km
3. Great Western Railway (G.W.R.), with a track length of . . . . 6,102 km
4. Southern Railway (S.R.), with a track length of . . . . 3,515 km

Total track length: 31,048 km.

Urban transport for London is run by the London Passenger Transport Board.

The networks of all four companies radiate outwards from London. London is also the base for each company's management.

The railways are the spine of internal transport in England. State planning was absent from the beginning, so construction of the railways took place according to economic considerations alone. Consequently, despite its high overall density, the railway network has, just like the road network, developed very unevenly and does not always match military needs.

The **density** of the network reflects population density, which varies considerably.

The focus of the rail network in *southern England* shows a considerable bias towards London, by far the largest rail hub in Great Britain. Lines radiate outwards from here in all directions and spread over the countryside in a network with dense coverage. The major lines leading from London to central England and the west have four tracks for long stretches.

The rail network in *central England* is, like that of southern England, very dense, above all in the industrial triangle of Liverpool, Leeds, and Birmingham.

Due to the unfavourable natural conditions and sparse population, the railway network in *Wales* is very thin.

The extent of the railways in *Scotland* and the *north of England* varies considerably. In northern England, there is a dense network around Newcastle, and in Scotland the area between Glasgow and Edinburgh has a network with dense coverage. Otherwise, the mountainous nature of the other parts of northern England and, above all, Scotland has prevented the railways from spreading much here.

Capacity. Of the entire English railway network,
around   11,400 km (i.e. 1/3) are single-track,
   "   16,400 km (i.e. 1/2) are two-track,
   "   2,900 km (i.e. 1/10) are three-track and above.

Specifically, the stretches of line with three or more tracks are to be found on the lines radiating outwards from London.

All lines in England are standard gauge.

As well as having a railway network considerably more dense than that of Germany, England also has more stretches of line with two and, especially, three or more tracks. Track systems at stations, on the other hand, are less sophisticated than in Germany.

Apart from the mountainous area in the north and Wales in the west, Great Britain has only minor rises in terrain. Deep cuttings, embankments, and numerous relatively short tunnels have been used to avoid climbs, so that the lines everywhere allow high speeds to be reached. Tunnels have also been built under rivers and in large towns.

The small width of the island means that the north–south lines have the greatest importance. London's early development as the main hub has further magnified this trend. Direct links across the island are relatively rare in England.

In 1937, the **rolling stock** of the four English railway companies was as follows:

steam locomotives	19,700
electric locomotives	13
passenger coaches	42,800
baggage coaches	17,800
goods wagons	639,800
(of which 45,000 can carry over 20 tonnes)	
private goods wagons	638,000

Thus, for every 100 kilometres there are

63 steam locomotives (Germany: 39)

138 passenger coaches (": 107)
2,064 goods wagons (": 1000)
2,058 private goods wagons (": 64)

With respect to the large number of goods wagons, it should be noted that most have a capacity of only 8 to 12 tonnes.

Electrification has taken place to a very small extent. The reason for this lies in the large amounts of coal available. Only the Southern Railway has electrified a meaningful part of its lines (900 kilometres in 1937). These stretches are supplied with power by a single generating plant, Lots Road (on the Thames above Chelsea).

Vulnerability to disruption. The individual sections of the English rail network offer excellent opportunities for disruption because of their many embankments, underpasses, and bridges, as well as the numerous short tunnels. The remarkable density of the rail network, however, makes long-lasting universal disruption of rail traffic near-impossible: diversions or alternative routes will almost always be available. The following are important rail junctions whose destruction will have far-reaching implications for rail traffic:

Newport (and the Severn Tunnel). All routes from the mining and industrial region of south Wales converge here.

Crewe is one of the most significant junctions in all of England. Many of the railway lines between London and the industrial area of central England converge here.

Leeds, one of England's most important junctions.

Carlisle and Newcastle. The only two lines between England and Scotland pass through here. It is no exaggeration to say that destruction of these two stations would interrupt all rail traffic between Scotland and England.

3. Inland Waterways

The horizontal and vertical layout of England provides extremely good conditions for the development of an effective system of waterways: no point on the island is more than 120 kilometres from the coast, and the low watersheds are easily overcome, allowing the individual river systems to be linked without great effort. For much of their length, the rivers themselves have the character of lowland rivers that lose height gently. Furthermore, the high quantities of precipitation mean that water levels are always fairly high.

Despite the favourable natural conditions, the modern waterway system is practically meaningless. The canals themselves are numerous, but most of them originated in the eighteenth century and have been heavily neglected, sometimes even fallen into disrepair, since the development of the railway network. In general, it can be said that the canals are, with very few exceptions, no wider than 20 metres and rarely deeper than 1.8 metres. The banks have been insufficiently strengthened, and the number of locks is far too great for modern transport. (See PLATES 1 AND 31)

As stated above, the inland waterways take only 5.4 per cent of all internal traffic.

The **Manchester Ship Canal** from Liverpool to Manchester is the only canal to have been improved into a modern shipping route. It alone carries almost half of all internal shipping.

4. Coastal Shipping

Coastal shipping naturally plays a significant role in England. Its rise has been aided remarkably by the many ports, the fact that the mouths of the rivers allow ocean-going vessels to travel far inland, and the fact that nowhere is more than 120 kilometres from the coast.

Coastal shipping carried around 50 to 65 million tonnes, around 20 per cent of the amount transported by rail.

POPULATION AND SOCIAL CONDITIONS

Population distribution displays striking contrasts that are becoming more pronounced with the course of time.

As one would expect, the highest **levels of population density** are to be found in the industrial regions; there are substantial areas here where a square kilometre is home to over 200 and sometimes as many as 1,000 people. Average levels of 50 to 100 per square kilometre are typical of the less heavily industrialized agricultural regions of average and better quality, but levels below 50 are to be found in areas where farming is the only activity, even those with good soil (as in East Anglia, strips of low-lying land in the north-east, etc.). Population density is particularly low (from under 25 to under 10) in the mountainous parts of the country. They are being abandoned, just like the areas given over to farming, as people leave the countryside for the dense settlements on the periphery of the industrial regions. At present, 80 per cent of the entire population lives in towns and cities, and only 20 per cent in the country.

In relation to these figures and the changes in the industrial sector they suggest, it is to be noted that the old concentrations are no longer expanding but actually in definite decline, while the commercially and administratively orientated major urban centres, above all London and its surroundings, continue to grow.

The largest **centres of population** are as follows (1931):

1. London with its suburban settlements and dependent towns: approximately 10 million (i.e. a quarter of the entire population of England and Wales).

46

2. Manchester and its satellite towns: 2.5 million.
3. Birmingham: 1.9 million.
4. West Yorkshire (Leeds–Bradford): 1.4 million.
5. Merseyside (Liverpool with Birkenhead, Wallassey, etc.): 1.3 million.
6. Tyneside (Newcastle, etc.): 1.1 million.
7. South Yorkshire (Sheffield): 0.5 million.

England is also a land of opposites in **social respects**. The impact of this, however, is softened by the widespread emergence of similarities in lifestyle; and the differences, because they are considered traditional, do not have such a divisive effect as they would in less conservative countries.

The not inconsiderable upper class consists of rich families as well as the old and new aristocracy, whose assets together make up the main part of the nation's wealth. Next, with its own elaborate internal hierarchy, comes the extensive working middle class, whose members enjoy sizeable incomes and considerable prosperity; in general, they have a considerably more comfortable lifestyle but lower level of education than in Germany.

There is also a lower class, fairly substantial in size, of workers on poor to average pay and the long-term unemployed, who have a surprisingly low material and intellectual standard of living. They inhabit the 'slums' (homes of misery) with their poor sanitary conditions, filth, and at times morbid forms of social existence (e.g. child poverty), in a state of poor health and in some cases long-term malnutrition. Some of these negative developments must be put down not to undeserved poverty but wholly or in part to insufficient competence in domestic matters, specifically among women, as well as to a lack of mutual encouragement.

The most striking features displayed by the more disagreeable sections of this class include a lack of personal ambition, indifference to the demands of community and nation, and interests that stop with sport and frivolity, the sensations of city life.

In some cases one is dealing here with the residue of an urban social group that has already been making its presence felt for over a hundred years and whose numbers already make up an alarming proportion of the population as a whole.

Racially, the population is a mixture of Mediterranean, Alpine, and Nordic elements, with the latter predominant.

The west of England, above all Wales, is home to remnants of an indigenous population whose roots go back to Celtic times and beyond. Unlike the bright English, they are dark and small in stature. Even though they have largely abandoned their language, they have still retained a reasonably strong awareness of the distinctive heritage and culture to which they belong. Radical political aspirations are confined to narrow circles and are of no practical significance.

PART 2
Strategic and Military Assessment

OVERALL EVALUATION

As far as **troop movements** are concerned, generally favourable conditions will be found in the *eastern lowlands*. The ridges here, too, are readily traversed, especially eastwards and westwards, less so northwards and southwards because of the obstacles posed by the many intervening valleys. There is an admirably well developed network of roads and tracks whose coverage is remarkably extensive even on the ridges of high ground. Only in the marshy areas of some estuaries and parts of the coast are significant gaps to be found; motorized units will encounter difficulties here.

The *mountainous zone of the west*, on the other hand, invariably presents difficult conditions for troop movements; there are places where passage is impossible except along certain narrow corridors. Mountain units would be needed to take parts of Wales and the mountains of Cumberland. There are large areas where roads are infrequent.

Obstacles of a special kind are presented by the extensive *housing estates*, factories, and other complexes in the cities and industrial towns, which place severe constraints on the mobility of motorized units in extensive areas.

Further obstacles to be mentioned include the *stone walls* and *hedgerows* with which fields and pastures are marked out in most parts of England. The system of hedgerows varies considerably in density, which is generally greatest in the fertile depressions of the lowlands.

These hedges and walls provide good **sources of cover**, but not, however, against attack from the air. A limited amount of cover is provided by the many small patches of woodland and coppices, especially the parkland; more substantial cover is to be found in the numerous and extensive settlements that exist in large concentrations or diffuse masses on the one hand and are spread out as scattered communities across the flatlands and the lower parts of the mountains on the other.

The steep sides of the ridges, which often extend for considerable distances, offer natural **vantage points** of the highest standard. There is no shortage of vantage points in the mountains, but, even so, first-class observation points are relatively scarce because of the frequent plateau-like nature of the land. The ground surveyed does not usually extend beyond short sections of valley.

In all of England, but particularly in the west, **visibility** is severely and very often reduced, often for extensive periods of time, by mist, fog, cloud, and drizzle.

The steep sides of the lowland ridges offer excellent **natural positions**. As most of them face inland, however, they are more favourable to an enemy attacking from the east, south, or south-east than to the defender. Because of their small size, the rivers do not offer any outstanding opportunities for obstruction or dividing the ground, except where they widen in their lower reaches to estuaries, usually flanked by soft ground that is hard to cross and liable to flooding. Some rivers burst their banks after persistent rain and thus become natural obstacles of a more significant nature.

Those constructing **field fortifications** will encounter difficulties in various low-lying parts with a high water table, on the heights of the escarpments with a shallow surface layer, and on the saturated turf of the mountain tops. On the other hand, the firm and dry rock of the lowland ridges is particularly suited to the construction of elaborate fortifications. This potential has been exploited in the case of several coastal fortifications. It is imperative to note regarding all kinds of trench-building that, in the area where limestone is widespread, excavated earth will be white and therefore visible from afar, especially so from the air. Any damage to the surface of the earth must be carefully concealed.

Billeting troops will be easily possible throughout the reasonably well to densely populated lowlands, and the productive agricultural areas of eastern and central England will make a substantial contribution to **provisions**. In the case of the large urban conglomerations, this can probably be expected only in the event of a surprise occupation that prevents storehouses and the like from being emptied or destroyed. The mountains of the west, on the other hand, with their extremely thin and scattered population, have very little to offer in either respect.

A similar contrast exists with respect to all other **supplies**. The scarcity of forests means that a severe shortage of wood must be expected throughout England. The trees that do grow there are mainly oaks and other broad-leafed varieties that are difficult to process. Because of the industrialized society and the dense population with its high level of consumption, supply sources of all kinds are present in abundance in all large settlements. Only in the case of rapid action, however, will it be possible to secure them intact.

THE INDIVIDUAL REGIONS

1. South-west England (Devon and Cornwall)

South-west England is an isolated, poorly accessible part of England with a distinctive regional character.

The **coastline** consists mainly of inaccessible rocky cliffs worn away by the sea. Nonetheless, on the southern side in particular, the fjord-like mouths of several valleys provide excellent natural harbours that lack only effective lines of communication with the interior. Examples: Falmouth, Plymouth, Dartmouth–Kingswear, Exmouth, Teignmouth–Devonport. The latter two suffer from heavy sedimentation as a result of river action, as do the similar but less numerous estuary harbours on the northern side (Barnstaple–Bideford).

The **population** is of Celtic descent; only in eastern Devon and the harbours is it intermingled with Saxon and Scandinavian elements respectively. The Celtic language may have died out, but the inhabitants have nonetheless retained a strong sense of belonging and an awareness of their distinctive heritage, which expresses itself in the form of reticence towards outsiders. The river Tamar marks the eastern boundary of the area inhabited by pure Celtic stock. Population density is unimpressive, ranging from roughly 50 to around 100 in the catchment areas around the towns.

Military Evaluation

The **possible landing sites** are confined to a small number of harbour areas, most of which have been fortified against attack. Attempts to **assemble significant troop concentrations**, as well as the dispersion and **movement** of such forces, will meet with difficulty where billeting and provisioning are concerned, and when faced with the region's dissected landscape. The coastline, valleys, and hill ranges provide good defensive positions. The changing height of the ground restricts the area that can be observed from any given point; in favourable weather, though, the higher eminences offer views of a considerable distance, albeit rarely of every area in every direction. The most important centres are vulnerable to operations by naval forces.

2. Central Southern England

This region has a varied landscape and is everywhere a sought-after haven for the rich, retired officers and civil servants, and other settlers and holidaymakers (Bournemouth in particular).

Military Evaluation

The **potential landing sites** are far more promising in the eastern part of the region than in the western part, which has no good harbours. **Troop movements** in a south–north direction and vice versa can be directed relatively easily across a broad front. The road network is dense. Off-road travel in the higher part of the region is hampered only by a network of widely separated hedgerows. **Sources of cover** in the form of hedges and patchy woodland are fairly plentiful in the Hampshire Basin and on the western section of the hills; the hedges also cover the entire Somerset plain.

The steep northern edge of the hills offers excellent **vantage points**, as do the isolated groups of hills in Somerset (the Quantock and Mendip Hills) and commanding eminences in the southern part of the region.

Natural positions and barriers are formed above all by the lines of hills running parallel to the coastline in the south (Purbeck, the Isle of Wight, behind Portsmouth). The steep edge of the central ridge constitutes a strong north-facing position. In Somerset, mention must be made not only of the isolated massifs but also of the marshy depressions of the Parret and the Brue, which block approaches to Bristol from the south.

Fortifications protect, above all, the area of Wight, Portsmouth, and Southampton, as well as Portland–Weymouth.

The entire region is widely settled and agriculturally productive, and therefore highly promising where **billeting** and **provisions** are concerned, even for more substantial numbers of troops; only the areas of truly high ground are an exception.

In summary, the central southern part of England must be considered an important, geographically favourable gateway to the heart of the island.

3. South-east England

The steep slope of the **North Downs**, which reaches 200 metres above sea level for much of its length, is accompanied in its northern and western parts by another sandstone ridge to the south. The highest point on either ridge, 294 metres, is to be found near Guildford on the north-western part of the latter. This second ridge spreads out to become broader in the west and is still heavily wooded (with deciduous trees as well as a large number of conifers). These two ridges, separated by a valley running between them, form a natural south-facing defensive position for London, one whose strength is increased by the fact that there are several places where one ridge makes up for a gap in the other. This twofold range of hills is at its narrowest and lowest between Guildford and Aldershot (only 30 metres high), where a broad low-lying area begins to spread out to the south.

The South Downs come to an end at Eastbourne. From there, the coastline is flat until the central hills meet the sea at Hastings as a 160 metre-high ridge. There follow the wetlands of Romney Marsh (including Dungeness), separated from the interior by a steep incline. Subsequently, imposing cliffs, 150 metres in height, are formed once more by the chalk escarpment of the North Downs. They watch over the fortress port of Dover, the 'key to England', nestled in its sheltered valley.

Military Evaluation

The harbours that present themselves for use in a **landing** are naturally protected by high cliffs. The harbours of the South Downs are most suitable, as here the cliffs are absent or less significant and the gentle south-facing slope of the Downs is exposed, with almost no sources of cover, to operations by naval forces, yet invisible from the interior. In addition, the steep north-facing slope of the Downs here provides those attacking from the south with an advantageous secure starting point from which the low-lying ground to the north can be surveyed. The indentations of many penetrating valleys, however, mean that the ridge is easily crossed.

Apart from the South Downs, the most important natural **defensive lines** are formed by the double barrier of the High Weald and the North Downs. In both instances, patches of woodland provide very good **sources of cover** in places.

The **rivers** do not pose any significant obstacles. Turning the lines of defence mentioned above in a movement along the east–west axis will be complicated by the incisions made by the many intervening valleys. The best chance for an advance in such a direction is to be found at the foot of the North Downs, along the ancient Watling Street linking Canterbury and Chatham. Even here, of course, effective lines of resistance are formed by the river Stour, the wooded area west of Canterbury, and the lower Medway with the fortified complex of Rochester, Chatham, and Gillingham.

The greatest natural weakness in the barriers listed above lies to the south-west of London, in the Guildford Gap, where the North Downs are reduced to a narrow ridge only 30 metres high and the High Weald comes to its western end.

The many orchards and hop gardens of northern Kent play a special role as sources of **cover**.

The area is densely settled and therefore well suited to the **billeting** of troops. Its agricultural richness will prove helpful in contributing to the supply of **provisions**.

4. The London Basin

The London Basin is bounded by the Chiltern Hills to the north, Reading to the west, and the North Downs or the High Weald to the south. Its population has everywhere, to some extent or another, merged with that of London itself. The more heavily built-up urban area displays a strong industrial presence in its northern, eastern, and southern parts; they are generally distinct from the commercial and administrative centre of the City and the purely residential districts of the western sector. Only in the heart of the city have high-rise buildings been constructed; further away from the core, lines of identical houses stretching monotonously across the landscape are everywhere the norm.

The **Thames** begins to widen as soon as it enters London. It is 400 metres wide in the City and reaches 800 metres in the East End. Downstream from the Tower, the docks extend continuously as far as Woolwich. Huge gristmills, gasworks, electric power stations, oil storage plants and refineries, and cement and paper factories line the river here and further downstream. The estuary proper begins after Gravesend (35,500 inhabitants); pilots are picked up here. The main oil storage plants are located in Thameshaven and Shellhaven on the north bank below Gravesend. Numerous old port towns, harbours, and industrial settlements are to be found along the estuary. An important secondary urban centre consisting of Rochester, Chatham, Gillingham, and Sheerness (over 160,000 inhabitants combined) has developed on the Medway estuary, where the Navy has shipyards, workshops, and warehouses. Mechanical industry, paper and cement production, engine manufacturing, seaplane factories, and chemical plants (poison gas) are also to be found here.

Military Evaluation
There are three major factors to be taken into account as major obstacles where **troop movements** in a south–north direction are concerned: (1) the broad Thames estuary, in places widened still further by soft ground with few roads and guarded by numerous fortifications; (2) the huge conglomeration of London, whose central districts, moreover, have narrow streets that are constantly clogged

with traffic; and (3) the upper Thames, which is still wide enough to present considerable difficulties if heavy troops attempt to cross it.

The west-east line formed by these three obstacles has the potential to play an important role as a **major defensive barrier**. Its strength is increased by the lines of hills to the north; they run from south-west to north-east and also serve as important **vantage points**.

Likewise, London, the lines of hills mentioned above, and the course of the river Lea all form a significant barrier running in an east-west direction.

5. The Ridges of Central England

This is a mainly agricultural transitional region between the London Basin and the capital on the one hand and the industrial Midlands on the other. The upper Thames Basin or **Oxford Basin** is divided into two longitudinal basins by an intervening limestone ridge broken down into separate hills (up to 170 metres). The famous ancient university town of Oxford (80,500 inhabitants) serves an extensive catchment area and lies on the Thames where it breaks through this intervening ridge.

Arable and cattle farming are both popular; the Oxford Basin and the Kennet valley, in particular, have adapted to dairy farming. The limestone heights are, as usual, generally used as grazing land for sheep, even if fields are becoming more common.

Military Evaluation

Apart from some particularly high steep drops, the area poses no significant difficulties to **troop movements**. The coverage of the road and rail network is generally very good.

LEGEND

Publisher's note: The below legend has been compiled from the different maps used to avoid repetition. Not all symbols on the maps appear in the original map legends. Annotated entries appear below each individual map, numbered non-consecutively as the originals. The index for each map appears at the back of the book.

(A) Individual symbols

⚡	Power station	▦	Pumping station
⚒	Iron foundry	⛽	Oil mill
★	Cultural monument, art gallery	⚡	Factory producing electrical goods
⊕	Hospital, military hospital	⊏	Copperworks
✉	Post office	Ⓐ	Chemical plant, chemical industry
⚑	Barracks, military encampment	⬮	Fat processing
⚑	Ammunition dump	⬮	Beer
▼	Fuel storage, refuelling station	▣	Printing
⬛	Railway facility, railway works, locomotive works, station facilities	⬛	Cattle market
⬛	Warehouse, silo, animal food store, grain silo, goods shed, covered market	⬮	Lorry and goods wagon factory
⬛	Gasworks	Ⓒ	Car-tyre factory
⬛	Mill	Ⓟ	Paper industry
⬛	Coal storage	⬮	Electrical technology laboratory
⬮	Aircraft engine manufacture	⬮	Military transmission post
⬮	Car factory, bodywork plant	⚓	Harbour area (quay, dock), port facilities, loading area
⬮	Machine works, engine factory	⬮	Dry dock, ship repair, shipyard, wharf, dockyard
⬮	Iron industry	⋈	Rail bridge
⬮	Textile Industry	⋈	Road bridge
⬮	Sawmill, wood storage, timber-yard	—	Footbridge
⬮	Cement works	) (	Tunnel
		)==(	
		∨	Lock, weir

(B) Other elements

(I) Thick lines: (General, for all maps)
━━━━ Thick lines mark the outline of larger features.

(II) Magnetic north:
Data is present only on a couple of legends, namely Figs.1 and 2. (the same for each).

Grid magnetic angle for mid-1940.
At the centre of the sheet, magnetic north is roughly 10° 30' west = 186.7 west of grid north on the **Gauß-Krüger grid**.
Annual decline: 10' or 2.96.

Fig 1. **Holborn**

Fig 2. **Westminster**

Fig 3. **Bermondsey**

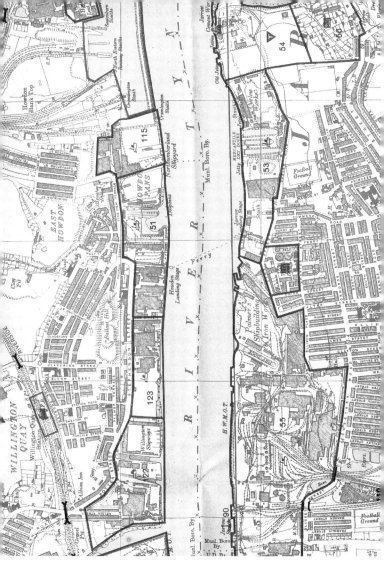

Fig 4. **South Shields**

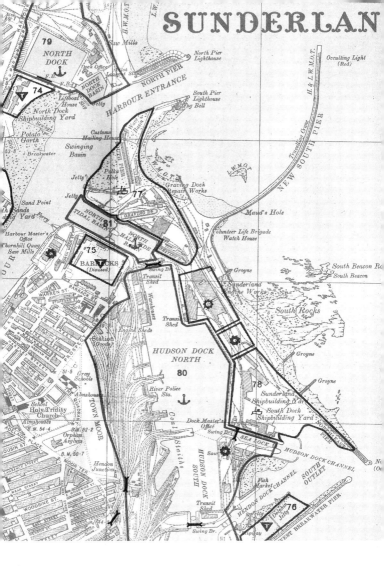

Fig 5. **Sunderland**

Fig 6. **Liverpool**

Fig 7. **Manchester**

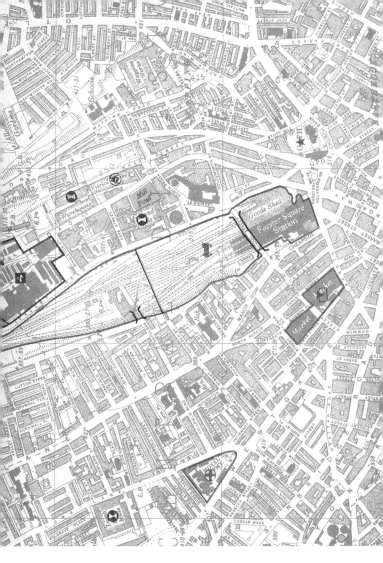

Fig 8. **Bradford**

Fig 9. **Derby**

Fig 10. **Leeds**

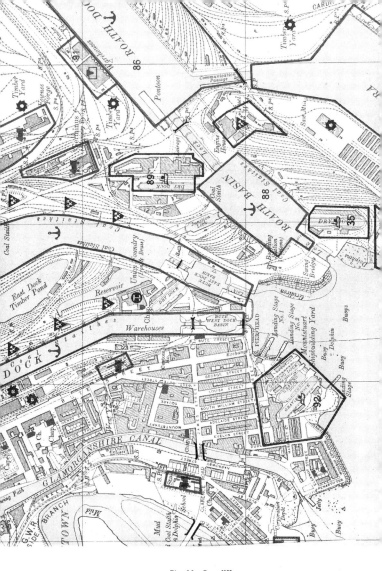

Fig 11. **Cardiff**

Fig 12. **Oxford**

Fig 13. **Coventry**

Fig 14. **Birmingham**

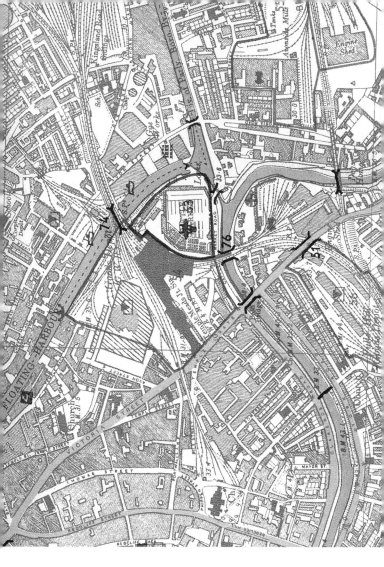

Fig 15. **Bristol**

With their escarpments, the lines of hills form important natural **defensive areas**. In those places where the escarpments are particularly pronounced, the advantage lies clearly with troops operating in a north-westerly direction, as they will be able to occupy strong positions here that also dominate the low-lying ground beyond.

Nowhere do the **rivers** present a substantial obstacle. There are no marshy areas of significant size.

Here again we have a region split into longitudinal sections that are themselves divided, specifically by the many transverse valleys through the ridges, as well as by the rising ground and indentation of the upper Ouse valley in the central plain.

Sources of cover are confined almost solely to parkland and hedges and therefore insignificant in overall terms. They are almost entirely absent in the north-east.

Finding **billeting and provisions** for troops should generally be easy.

6. The Fens

At around 4,000 square kilometres the Fenland is the only true **plain** of any considerable size in England. The **population** is divided between medium-sized villages (on the islands and higher silt deposits), linear and single-street settlements, and some small market towns. Population density is generally somewhere above 50 per square kilometre. There is no industry apart from brickworks around Peterborough. The water supply system is not good: the villages obtain their water from shallow wells, and the towns use filtered river water.

Military Evaluation

The numerous dykes and drainage ditches pose an obstacle to **troop movements**. In addition, many areas are liable to flooding.

Sources of cover are very scarce (few clusters of trees, settlements).

Insufficient **vantage points** are available on the ground (church towers).

The region is well placed to provide **provisions** for troops.

7. East Anglia

East Anglia is a purely agricultural region; mixed farming is the norm, with the emphasis on crop production. Dairy farming (with Friesian cattle) is confined to the moist low-lying ground. **Transport** faces hardly any significant obstacles and is, apart from the Harwich line, of purely regional importance.

Military Evaluation

The landscape and nature of the ground are such that even heavy motorized units will find movement straightforward. The only major **divisions** are those formed by the brief drop to the west and the courses of the valleys running in a west–east to north-west/south-east direction, and of them only the sections near the sea present serious obstacles (soft ground liable to flooding, expanses of water).

Apart from the wooded areas of the Breckland and the Sandlings, **sources of cover** are unsatisfactory. There is a lack of **vantage points**. Only three ports, Lowestoft, Yarmouth, and Harwich, are available for **landings** of a substantial nature. The coast is well suited to defence.

The situation regarding **billeting and provisions** is favourable.

8. Wales

The extensive mountainous land of Wales creates a barrier between central England and the Irish Sea that can be crossed only with difficulty. It is also a sheltered haven where remnants of the ancient Celtic population have survived; their influence on the land in racial and in part also cultural respects can be felt even today. With the exception of the mining area of south Wales, the whole region is of little economic significance, and is moreover very thinly populated. For these reasons it does not come into consideration as a base for significant numbers of troops.

Apart from south Wales and the peripheral mining area of north-east Wales, Wales is to all intents and purposes a purely agricultural region. Forest cover is extremely sparse. As befits the damp climate, **grazing** is by far the main use made of the land: the upland moorland areas are given over to sheep in summer (they too are brought down to lower levels in winter), and the fields serve mostly as permanent pasture where cattle and horses are raised. Only 15 to 20 per cent of cultivated land is used for growing oats and animal feed. Beef cattle are reared in the north-west, with more dairy cattle in the south-west.

The Welsh nationalist movement has been on the rise again for some time; it is, however, far more cultural than political in nature.

Military Evaluation

Wales, with the considerable **difficulties posed by its terrain**, is an ideal region in which to mount a persistent defence; internal **lines of communication**, however, are scarce. The main link between north and south hugs the coastline. Motorized units can operate here only with great difficulty.

Only a very small number of troops can be **billeted** in Wales, and access to **provisions** here is limited. Supplying and regrouping troops will be hampered by the scarcity of good harbours.

Sources of cover are modest due to the shortage of forest.

9. The Mining Area of South Wales

The southern mining area is by far the most economically important part of Wales. It is also home to around 1.6 million of the 2.65 million people that make up the population of the entire country (including Monmouthshire).

Coal extraction is based in the valleys, which are now filled with long streams of **workers' housing** and mining shafts. Exploitation of the deposits progressed from east to west, moving from bituminous coal east of the Taff valley to 'steam coal' (centred on Rhondda with its 141,000 inhabitants), and on to anthracite (west of the Neath valley). Accordingly, it is in the east that one finds the worst living and working conditions — numerous small pits next to one another, often with partially obsolete equipment.

In addition to the Welsh core, a large number of immigrants from outside can be identified in the **population**. With no ties to the land, they constitute a restless element.

Military Evaluation

Motorized units in this area will be dependent on the road network, which is fairly dense. Surveying the land is widely impossible. The steep south and south-east flanks of the hills impede operations, as do the deep and steeply carved valleys. Ample landing opportunities are provided by the coal ports.

Billeting possibilities exist, but are hardly promising. The provisions to be obtained from the area itself are of no significance.

10. The Monmouth and Hereford Hills

A **combination of various landscapes** including rolling plains, hills, furrowed valleys, and massifs rising rather abruptly to between 300 and 400 metres in height.

The favourable climate (relatively little precipitation and mild temperatures), together with the fertile red soil, means that the Hereford plain and its surroundings are a good **area for arable farming**. In addition to oats (the main crop), wheat, barley, and sugar beet are grown. Together with the Worcester region to the east, this is the second most important hop-growing region in England. Fruit is also extensively cultivated, and the orchards are just as characteristic of the landscape here as they are in Kent.

Military Evaluation

Troop movements of any kind are entirely feasible in the Hereford area. Few **sources of cover**.

Rich in **vantage points** and commanding high ground.

Important **barriers** running from north to south are formed by (1) the line of the Malvern Hills and the Forest of Dean and (2) the edge of the Welsh mountains. These barriers are intersected by lines of high and low ground running from south-west to north-east. The transverse valley of the Wye is significant in the Forest of Dean.

The region would seem to be a suitable source of **provisions** for troops because of the good arable farming conditions.

11. The Midlands

The Midlands are part of England's ancient industrial heartland. Industrialization first took place on the foundations provided by deposits of iron ore, other sources of raw materials, and a multitude of small coalfields. By adapting to host modern industries as well, the region has avoided the stagnation typical of more northern parts.

Agriculture in the Midlands is dominated by cattle farming, above all dairy farming. In particular, permanent pasture is by far most common on the low-lying ground with heavy soil. Cattle farming is particularly strong in Cheshire (famous cheese) and northern Shropshire, also in Worcestershire and further south, as well as in Warwickshire and northwards.

Military Evaluation

Even away from its dense road network, the region poses few obstacles to **troop movements** of any kind in any direction, apart from the large urban and industrial conglomerations. The hedges have a role to play here too, of course. There are also fairly short stretches of the Trent, Severn, Dee, and Mersey that are vulnerable to flooding and have the potential to pose difficulty.

Particularly obvious natural obstacles and positions are to be found above all in the mountains and ridges bordering the region, as well as in the steeply rising north-eastern outliers of the Welsh mountains at Ironbridge. The parallel outliers of the Pennine Hills give the appearance of being a second barrier more than they actually are. The military significance of the central hilly areas and swellings in the landscape is equally negligible, though somewhat increased by forest cover in places.

The **vantage points** on the edge of the surrounding mountains offer views extending more or less far into the distance, as do some points on the central area of higher ground.

The dense settlement means that hardly any difficulties present themselves where the **billeting** of troops, even in large numbers, is concerned; the agricultural situation in the region, however, is such that it can make only a partial contribution to **provisions**.

12. The Lancashire Lowlands and Industrial Area

This region contains one of the largest concentrations of industry in England because of the coal that has accumulated near the surface around the slopes of Rossendale. Mining operations are extending away from the edge of the hills and onto the plain with the help of deeper and deeper shafts.

Manchester is the prototypical example of an old English industrial town with an extensive belt of slums that presents a serious problem. The unpleasant consequences of the post-war crisis have brought about a partial transition to modern light industry and armament production in this industrial area and that of the Ribble.

Military Evaluation

The **Mersey**, which runs between Manchester and Liverpool, poses significant obstacles in the form of its wide estuary on the one hand and the extensive wet moorland of the Chat Moss on the other. Between them, the middle section of the river from Widnes to Warrington, also skirted by higher ground to the north and south, is more easily crossed.

To a lesser extent, the **Ribble** and the **Lune** should also be noted as **barriers** between the mountains and the sea.

Troop movements in the industrial area are partly helped by the density of the road network, but partly hindered by the many factory buildings and settlements.

The rich agricultural lowlands will be able to make a sizeable contribution to **provisions** for a unit.

13. The Pennine Hills

This group of mountains, 200 kilometres in length, forms the spine of northern England. It is not a chain but a **coherent series of relatively low massifs** that have more or less retained their elevated plateaux despite the incisions of the valleys. In places, the mountain group forms an effective barrier to communications between east and west; in some cases, considerable effort is needed to traverse or breach it. At other points, it can be crossed without difficulty.

Population density in the mountains is very low. Settlements are confined to the valleys, as are the few fields. Sheep are extensively reared for meat, and this constitutes the main branch of the region's economy. Horses and cattle are rare. People are emigrating from the mountains, except where industrial settlements encroach from the west or east.

The **military significance** of the region follows directly from the information presented above.

14. Leeds and Sheffield: The Industrial Region East of the Pennines (Western Yorkshire)

Like its counterpart in Lancashire, this region has become an industrial centre due to the presence of coal. Mining has led to a general increase in **population** density; the large concentrations are the result of **industry**. The following areas can be identified:

1. The district home to the wool industry in the West Riding with Leeds at its centre (a mass of around 1.3 million people in total). This area extends southwards to include Huddersfield and Wakefield. There is a fairly even balance between weaving and spinning, both of varying quality.

2. The steel industry is concentrated in and around Sheffield (512,000 inhabitants); the focus is less on smelting and steel production (around Rotherham, 70,000 inhabitants) than on the manufacture of knives and small steel products of top quality. Also present are mechanical industry, chromium works, armament production, and so on.

3. Vehicle manufacture is important in Derby (142,400 inhabitants) and Nottingham (269,000 inhabitants) on the southern edge of the area; also widespread here is, above all, the production of knitwear, hosiery, and lace.

Military Evaluation

The gentle contours of the region permit troop movements of all kinds; the course of the damp, awkward U-shaped valleys is such that movement is easier in an east-west direction in the north, and easier in a north-south direction in the south. Short steep slopes before the mountains will also be encountered here.

15. The Lowlands of North-east England (Central Yorkshire)

This strip of low ground, 30 kilometres in width, is the north-eastern extension of the lowlands of central England. It has a pronounced eastern boundary in the form of a series of inclines that extend northwards as a continuation of the hills of central England. To the north, the area gradually gives way to that of the Tees.

The region consists of fertile meadow-ground or, in somewhat higher parts, of glacial deposits. Climatically, the region is among the drier parts of England. Thus, in addition to pasture, **arable farming** plays a considerable role (wheat, potatoes, barley, sugar beet). Beef cattle are fattened on the lush meadows. The region is one where large-scale farms are predominant.

Military Evaluation

The region is of great **significance** because it is part of the north-south artery of communication on which Britain depends.

Sections with patches of bog and areas liable to flooding make the north-south line formed by the Ouse and the Trent more important than the size of the rivers themselves would suggest.

The region is purely agricultural and can make a considerable contribution to troop **provisions**.

Sources of cover are available only insufficiently in parkland forests, scattered groups of trees, hedges, and settlements.

16. The Ridges of North-east England (Eastern Yorkshire)

The landscape here, as in the preceding section, is a continuation of that of central England, in this case of the ridges whose escarpments there face north-west. Here, the steep sides point westwards, the gentle slopes eastwards or south-eastwards.

The **coastline** is smooth in parts, cliffed in others. It has few good harbours apart from the Humber estuary, which has seen considerable improvement and is now a first-class port area.

The only area of industrial significance is that of the Humber estuary with the large harbour town of Hull (313,000 inhabitants), Grimsby (92,500), and other settlements; in some cases, they provide access to the industrial and mining regions of the interior, in others they are bases for the fishing industry.

Military Evaluation

The **navigability** of the land in east–west and north–south directions varies across the region.

The escarpments provide strong west-facing **natural positions**. Accordingly, they favour a force attacking from the east — which would, of course, have few potential landing sites to choose from and find its advance impeded by a number of strips of moist land running from north to south. The Humber estuary permits the deployment of naval forces far inland.

Sources of cover are very scarce in this bare landscape. The situation regarding **billeting** and **sources of food** for troops is not unfavourable. Most other supplies (timber in particular) would have to be brought in from outside.

17. The Mountains of Cumberland

The mountains of Cumberland are a dome-like swelling, sharply dissected by steep-sided valleys spreading out in radial fashion from the centre, with ridges that still present the remnants of a high plateau. They rise to 950 metres. The numerous lakes make this mountain landscape particularly appealing; it attracts many visitors. A very difficult region for vehicle transport.

The small coalfield in the north-west, between Aspatria and Whitehaven (21,100 inhabitants), lends the region significance. In combination with the presence of iron ore around Cleator and Egremont (south-east of Whitehaven), the coal has led to the development of an iron and steel industry in Workington (24,700 inhabitants). This has been joined by mechanical and shipbuilding, above all in Workington and Barrow (66,400 inhabitants), where, in fact, submarines are constructed in the naval shipyards.

18. The Industrial Region of North-east England

This mining and industrial region is located on the eastern slope of the Pennine Hills, whose outliers here extend as far as the coastline. It consists of the Tyne and Wear valley basins and the broad plain around the Tees.

Deposits of iron ore in the Cleveland Hills stimulated the emergence of large iron- and steelworks on the Tees estuary that now process ore from elsewhere. In the cities on the Tyne, it is above all shipbuilding that has established itself as the main additional industry. This dependence means that the whole region is suffering under the new post-war conditions, above all the decline in coal exports. Attempts to revive the economy by introducing new industries and severe rationalization measures are underway and have been with carried out with some success.

Military Evaluation
The outliers of the Pennine Hills rise commandingly over the region. Specifically, Black Hill to the south of New Castle is significant. In the central area, in particular, the fairly widespread valleys present a number of hindrances to troop movements. The middle section of the Wear valley forms a fairly strong natural barrier that runs parallel to the coastline and continues northwards to the Tyne.

19. The Scottish Border
The region near the border with Scotland is filled mainly by the Cheviot Hills, whose character is entirely similar to that of the northern Pennines.

The outliers fall gradually towards the eastern coast; they are interrupted by a line of low ground running roughly from north to south that defines what could be described as a secondary chain, itself interrupted by the valleys of the Coquet and the Alu. Several militarily important divisions are created as a result. The main lines of communication with Scotland, however, are to be found on the outside of the region, running along the coast.

Sheep farming is the predominant activity throughout the region. The long-established wool industry has managed to survive by specializing in the production of 'tweed'. New industries, such as rayon, have also been introduced.

Population density is low in the mountains; it increases towards the coast.

The pool of resources that could be drawn on in obtaining **provisions** for a unit is modest.

PART 3
Important Military And Geographical Phrases With Pronunciation Guide

Linguistic Notes

English article: *the*, singular and plural, with voiced *th* (dh).
Plural formation: generally, add −s.
Voiced *th* is indicated by (dh), voiceless *th* by (th).
The stress mark (´) is placed before the stressed syllable.
å = sound between a and o.

Military Installations

German	English	Pronunciation
Bodenfunkstelle	aeronautical W/T	ähronåh'tikl dabl'ju-tie
Flughafen	aerodrome, air port	ährodrohm', ähr'port
Flughafenfeuer	aerodrome beacon	ährodrohm' bie'ken
Flugstreckenfeuer	airway beacon	ähr'ueh bie'ken
Funkfeuer	radio beacon	rä'dio bieken
Funkpeilstelle	aeronautical D/F	ähronå'htikl die-ef
Gebiet mit Sprengun-gen	explosives area	iksploh'siws ähria
Gefahrengebiet	danger area	dehn'dscher äh'ria
Kaserne	barrack	bär'räck
Luftfahrtfeuer	aerial light	äh'riäl lait
Luftnavigationsfeuer	air navigation beacon	ähr nävigeh'schen bie'ken
Militärlager	camp	kämp
Schießplatz	rifle range	raifl' rehndsch'
Sperrgebiet	prohibited area	prohi'bitid äh'ria
Verteidigungsturm aus älteren Zeiten	martello tower	martel'lo tau'er
Wasserflughafen	seaplane port	ßie'plehn port

Billeting and Provisions

German	English	Pronunciation
Bett	bed	bed
Brot	bread	bred
Butter	butter	bat'ter
Fleisch	meat	miet
Garage	garage	gär'ridsch
Hafer	oat	oht
Heu	hay	heh
Kaffee	coffee	kof'fie
Milch	milk	milk
Pferd	horse	håhß
Stall	stable	ßtehbl
Stroh	straw	ßtråh
Tee	tea	tie
Unterkunft	lodging	lod'sching
Wagen, Auto	motorcar	moh'torkahr
Wasser	water	uå'ter
Wurst	sausage	ßå'ßidsch

Miscellaneous

German	English	Pronunciation
Binnentief	pool	puhl
Blatt, Kartenblatt	sheet	schiet
drahtlos; Telephon	wireless	ueir'leß
gefährlich	dangerous, foul	dehn'dscheres, faul
Höhenlinien	contours	kontuhrs'
Kartennull b. Landkarten	ordnance datum	åh'dnänß dät'um
Kartennull bei Seekarten keine feststehende Be-ziehung zum Land-kartennull)	tidal datum	taidl dä'tum
Landkarte	map	mäp
Maßstab	scale	ßkehl

nicht beleuchtet	unlighted	an'laitid
rechtweisend	true	truh
Tiefenlinien	submarine contours	ßab'merain kontuhrs'

Klafter, Faden (= 1.83 m = unit of depth on English sea charts)
fathom   fä'dhim

Gallic Words

a	der, die, das	drucin	Bergrücken
abbuinn⎞ aven ⎠	Fluß	dubh, du	schwarz
		dun	Wall, Fort
aird⎞ ard ⎠	Höhe, Huk		
		ear	Ost
airidh	Fischerhütte	eileach, eilean	Insel, Inselchen
alet	kleiner Fluß Oder Bach	garbh	rauh
am⎞ an ⎟ ant⎠	der, die, das	geo, geodha	Bucht, Kriek
		glas	grün, grau
		gleann	enges Tal, Bergschlucht
		gob	Schnabel
baa	Fels, Klippe	gorm	blau
bad	Gehölz, Wäldchen	holm	kleine Insel
bagh	Bucht		
baile	Farm, Stadt	iar	West
ban, bhan	weiß	innus or inch	Insel mit Weideland
barr	Gipfel	klatch	Stein
bass	Fels, Klippe	klet	rauhe Anhöhe
beg	klein	knowe	Hügel
bealach	Paß, Spalte	krag	Küstenabhang
ben	Berg	kyle, kyllo	Sund
bhreac, breac	gesprenkelt	lag	Loch, Höhle
bhuidhe, buidhe	gelb	leac, lekh	Schiefer
bid	Gipfel	lia, liath	grau, blau
bo, bogba	blinde Klippe	linne, linsche	Bucht, Binnensee

79

bu	Klippe unter Wasser	loch	See
bun	Fluß, Flußmündung	lon	Fluß
camas, camus	Bucht, Kriek	maol	Vorgebirge
caol caolas	Föhrde, Sund	meall	Klumpen
ceann	Vorgebirge, Huk	more	groß
clach	Stein	mointeach	Moor
cleit	rauhe Anhöhe	monadh	
cnoc	Hügel	mol, moll	Küstenabhang
coire	Stromwirdel	mull	Vorgebirge
corran	Haken	mullach	Gipfel
creag	Küstenabhang	na	
crois	Kreuz	na la	
cruach	Hafen	nam	der, die, das
cul	schmal, eng	nan	
dearg	rot	ob, obe	Kriek. Hafen
deas	süd	oitir	Untiefe, flach
pal, poll, poul, puill	kleiner Teich, Bucht, Moor	sron	Vorgebirge, Kap
		stoe	steiler Fels,
rhu, ruadh	rot		spitzer Hügel
ru, rudha, rugh	Landspitze, Huk	strath	Flußtal
salann, salean	Salzwasserbucht	tob	Brunnen, Quelle
sgeir	Klippe	torr	spitzer Hügel
sgeirean	Klippen	traigh	sandiger Strand, Sand-bucht
sgon, sgonn	Klumpen		
sgor, sgurr	Bergspitze	tuath	Nord
sithean	Festland		
sloc	Grube, Höhle	uamh	Höhle

Welsh Words

aber	Flußmündung	moel	kahl, kegelförmiger Hügel
afon	Fluß		
bach, fach	klein	pen	Huk, hervorragender Platz
carreg ⎫ carrick ⎭	Fels, Klippe	pont	Brücke
clyt	Steinhaufen	porth	Hafen
		pwll	Sumpf, kleine Bucht
dau	zwei		
du	schwarz	sarn	Fußweg
isaf	niedriger, unterer		
llan	freier Platz, Kirche	traeth	Sandbank
llech	flacher Stein	trai	Strand bei Ebbe
maen	Stein, Fels	uchaf	oberer, höherer
mawr ⎫ fawr ⎭	groß	ymp	Insel

Model Questions

Welches ist der kürzeste Weg nach X?

Which is the shortest way to X?
uitsch ise schäh'test ueh tu X?

Gehen Sie geradeaus und biegen Sie dann nach links (rechts).

Go straight down and then turn to the left (right).
goh streht daun en dhen törn tu dhe left (rait).

Wie heißt diese Stadt?

What is the name of this town?
uät ise nehm ow dhis taun?

Wohin führt dieser Weg?

Where does this way lead?
uär dasis ueh lied?

Wo ist der nächste Tank?	Where is the next tank?
	uär ise nekßt tänk?
Wo ist die nächste Brücke?	Where is the next bridge?
	uär ise nekßt bridsch?
Wo ist das nächste Postamt?	Where is the next postoffice?
	uär ise nekßt pohßt'offiß?
Wo sind die Kasernen?	Where are the barracks?
	uär ahr dhe bärräcks?
Wo kann ich etwas zu essen bekommen?	Where can I get something to eat?
	uär kan ai get ßamthing tu iet?
Wo können wir schlafen?	Where can we sleep?
	uär kän uie ßliep?
Können Sie mir den Weg nach Y zeigen?	Can you show me the way to Y?
	kan juh schoh mi dhe ueh tu Y?

MONEY, WEIGHTS, AND MEASURES

Length:
1 English mile (mail) = 1,760 yards (jahds) = 1,609.34 m
1 English yard = 3 feet (fiet) at 12 inches (intchis) each
= 91.4 cm
1 ton = 1,016.06 kg
1 English inch = 2.54 cm

Area:
1 English acre (ehkr) = 160 square roads (ßkuähr rohds)
= 40.467 a

Volume:
1 barrel (barrel) = 163.5 l   1 gallon = 4.54 l

Conversion for English feet and metres
(1 foot = 0.304 794 494 metres)

Example: 1,237 feet, how many metres?
     1,000 feet = 304.79 metres
       200   "   = 60.96   "
        37 "   = 11.28   "

_____

    1237 feet = 377.03 metres

Weight:

1 hundredweight (hand´ridweht) = 4 quarters (kuå´ter)
each 2 stones (ßtohns), each 14 pounds = 50,800 kg

1 lb (*liber,* pound) = 453.6 g or 16 ounces (aunßis),
each 16 grams

Thus: 1 pound = 16 ounces

½	"	= 8	"
¼	"	= 4	"

Money

£	= 1 pound = 20 shillings (schillings)
1 crown (kraun)	= 2½ shillings
1 shilling	= 12 pence (penß)
1 penny	= 2 halfpenny (heh´peni)
1 halfpenny	= 2 farthings (far´dhings)
2 pennies	= twopence (tap penß)
3 pennies	= threepence (thrip´penß)
2 shillings 6 pence	= 2 sh. 6 d. or 2′ 6″

Overview of England's Industrial Areas

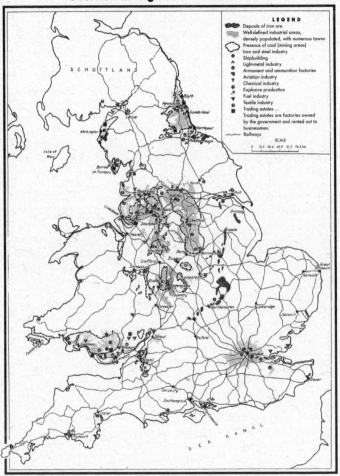

1940 edition

Army General Staff: Surveying and Military Mapping Section

INDEX TO MAPS

49 Royal Exchange
50 Bank of England
51 Stock Exchange
59 Greenland Dock, large cold-storage areas for storing dairy products. Greenland Dock primarily serves freighters from Canada (grain). Modern technical equipment, in particular in the machinery for unloading grain.
89 Tower Bridge (raising road bridge)
131 Cold store for frozen meat
228 London Bridge (passenger station)
229 Custom House
230 London Hospital, Whitechapel
231 London Dock Authority
236 Southwark Hospital

SOUTH SHIELDS
51 Tyne Improvements Commission, shipyard for repair work, mainly on dredgers and lighters
53 Mercantile Dry Dock Co., shipyard for repair work with three dry docks, a fitting-out quay 549 metres long; oil supply link with the neighbouring refuelling station
54 Refuelling station (Shell Mex. and Petr. Co.), fifteen tanks of various sizes; oil pier
55 Palmers Hebburn Co., shipyard, largely abandoned; repair work continues
56 Pumping station
90 Coal-loading facilities, Jarrow
115 Northumberland Shipbuilding Co., shipyard, completely abandoned
122 Chelands (Successors) Ltd, repair work; has two slipways
123 Tyne Iron Shipbuilding Co., shipyard, largely abandoned

SUNDERLAND
74 Refuelling station (bunker station of Power Petrol Ltd), five medium-sized tanks; oil pier
75 Refuelling station (bunker station) 3 medium-sized: 2 tanks, capacity around 7,000 t: oil supply links with Corporation Quay
76 Hendon Dock refuelling station (Shell Mex.), twelve medium-sized tanks, capacity around 20,000 t. Unloading of tankers is thought to take place in Hendon Dock.
77 Greenwell & Sons Ltd, repair workshops and port activity

78 Bartram & Sons Ltd, shipyard for the construction of merchant ships, rail link, capacity of 35,000 grt annually
79 North Dock, wood cargo is handled on the north-east side, oil cargo on the south-west side
80 Hudson Dock, transfer of mixed cargo, grain, coal (western staiths), and wood (eastern staiths) grain storage (around 10,000 t) Hendson Dock: transfer of wood, wood pulp, and oil
81 North Tidal Basin, ship fittings (eastern side), North Half Tide Basin: outer approach to Hudson Dock: docking of ships

LIVERPOOL
39 King Edward Hospital
40 Wool storage
41 Electric power station (steam and water)
42 Exchange Station (passengers and freight)
46 Technical school
71 Clarence Power Station at Trafalgar Dock
78 Grain store and oil mill at East Waterloo Dock, three granaries with a capacity of 30,000 t [t not expanded]
303 Nelson Dock, serves ships to Ireland and coastal shipping
304 Stanley Dock, coastal shipping
305 Collingwood Dock, coastal shipping (e.g. transport of building materials) to ports on the Bristol Channel and the south coast
306 Salisbury Dock, coastal shipping
307 Trafalgar Docks and Victoria Dock
308 Waterloo Docks, serves ships to Irish ports; grain storage
309 Princes Half Tide Dock, coastal shipping

MANCHESTER
143 Salford Electric, electrical goods production
171 Salford Station in western Manchester
173 Gas works in western Manchester

174 Copper works on the river Irwell in the Lower Broughton part of Manchester
176 Manchester General Post Office

BRADFORD
37 Electric power station, voltage: 66.33 kV; maximum load: 55,610 kW; overall performance in kW generator 88,500 transformer rectifier 28,180

DERBY
9 Midland Works, locomotive and wagon factory
10 Gas works

LEEDS
7 Steam, plough, and locomotive works: stamped steel: Airedale Foundry, cluster of steel and iron works
96 New Station (L.N.E.R. passenger station)
99 General Post Office
101 Monk Bridge Iron and Steel Works

CARDIFF
35 Commercial Dry Dock
48 Channel Dry Dock, with floating dock
86 Roath Dock
88 Roath Basin
89 Bute Dry Dock
91 Grain shed at Roath Dock
92 Mount Stuart Dry Docks 1-3

OXFORD
5 Town hall
7 University
8 Rail areas and rail works

COVENTRY
91 Morris Motors Ltd (Engines Branch), engine components and car parts
133 Coventry Motor Fittings Ltd, car fan production
136 Singer Motors Ltd, east and west works, car and aircraft engine factory
137 British Thomson Houston Comp, Ltd, aircraft engine factory

BIRMINGHAM
15 Saltley and Nettchell Gasworks
19 Saltley rail, lorry, and goods

23 Climax Tube Works
92 British Timken Ltd, iron foundry, ball bearing production
111 Electric & Ordenance Accessories Works
112 Paper factory (white and coloured paper)

BRISTOL
51 Bath Bridge (road)
54 Goods loading areas and cattle market at Temple Meads Joint Station
56 Large goods depots
63 Cattle market
76 New Cut Bridge